Father Figure

Books by
Beverley Nichols

My father, John Nichols. This sketch was made by a night nurse while he was sitting outside my mother's bedroom, waiting for her to die.

Father Figure ❧

Beverley Nichols

SIMON AND SCHUSTER
NEW YORK

To an Unknown Woman 🙰

When this book was finished I wondered to whom it might be dedicated. Then I remembered *Shadow of the Vine*.

This was a play of mine about a drunkard, and the havoc he wrought in the lives of those around him. Though the facts could not be narrated in all their naked brutality, the impact of the play was such that when it was produced on television my mail-bag was flooded with letters from all over the country. The great majority came from women, and they all asked the same question . . .

'How did you know so much about *my* life?'

Again and again these women, young or old, rich or poor, from every rank of society, none of whom I had ever met, demanded to be told how I had gained the knowledge that enabled me to put *their* tragedy on to the screen. Reading these letters I came to realize that my own dark background, which I had regarded as probably unique and certainly outdated, was in fact all too familiar to tens of thousands of families in our country today.

'Who told you about *my* husband and what he did to me and my children? Where did you learn what *we* had to go through when he had *delirium tremens*? How did you find out all the sickening little details – like standing on a chair to reach the bottles he had hidden on top of the wardrobe – like guiding his hand when he was too shaky to write a cheque?'

There was one letter, anonymous, that stood out from all the others; and perhaps it helped to persuade me to make public this tragedy of our times – for it is still a tragedy of our times. (There is no date to alcoholism; it was of the past, it is of the present, and it will be of the future.) The letter bore the postmark of Ilkley in Yorkshire, where, by a strange coincidence, my mother was born, over a century ago. It ended with the words . . . '*How did you know that there was murder in my heart?*'

This book is an answer to that question.

Chapter One ❧

The first time I remember my father he was lying dead drunk on the dining-room floor.

He had clutched the table-cloth as he fell, and the carpet was littered with silver, broken glass, fruit and spilled wine. A decanter of port which he had been holding had broken in his hand; there was blood flowing from his wrist, and it mingled with the wine which had drenched his shirt. My eldest brother, Paul, was trying to bind his wrist with a napkin. Paul was then twelve years old. My other brother, Alan, who had come running to fetch me out of bed, was nine.

I was six.

Lying there on the floor, with groans coming from his open lips, with his moustache dyed dark from the wine into which he had plunged his face, with his glazed eyes rolling to and fro, my father looked like a great animal that had been wounded in the chase. A dangerous animal too, who might get up, who might stagger about again, and bite and claw and kill.

As he lifted his head his eyes ceased to roll, and focused themselves slowly, relentlessly, on me. I wanted to run away, but my legs did not seem to belong to me. I could feel them shaking in my pyjama trousers. Still he stared, and suddenly he spat out a couple of words, in a strangled voice. I did not understand the words; at the age of six I was not so versed in obscene language as I was to become, under my father's tuition, at the age of nine. But I knew that the words boded no good. They were a threat from which I must escape. So I threw myself from my brother's arm and ran from the room, screaming in an agonized treble . . . 'Daddy's drunk, Daddy's drunk.'

II

In this book I must try not to let the vision be blurred by the miasma of hatred which, even to this day, seems to rise through the soil of his grave. For that grave is also my mother's resting-place, and it is her picture that I wish to paint. If only his image did not rise before me so constantly, getting in the way, like a slime over the canvas! That is an ugly phrase, reeking of hate. Can they be reconciled – the truth and the hatred? Are they one and the same?

Yes, they are, and both are stranger than fiction. I would not dare to write a novel in which a small boy behaved as I did then. The reader would condemn him as an intolerable little prig.

This is what happened.

I ran straight from the dining-room, through the hall, and down the long corridor past the billiards-room. I pushed open the swing door that led to the servants' hall. And I threw myself into the kitchen, where the cook was sitting over the fire, reading aloud to another maid.

'Daddy's drunk,' I kept crying. 'Daddy's drunk.'

The tears streamed down my face and my body would not stop trembling. I think that Alan had followed me and was trying to tell me not to say such things before cook. I cannot be quite sure, but I think so. The next moments are very clear indeed.

I fell on my knees by a kitchen chair, and prayed aloud. 'Oh, God . . . Daddy's drunk . . . please make him well.' The kindly, troubled face of the cook loomed over me, but I thrust her aside. 'Please, God, do not let him hurt my mother. Please make him well. Oh, God . . . Daddy's drunk . . . drunk.'

The face of the cook, and behind it, the face of the big

4

kitchen clock. The hard feel of the chair on my elbows. The rungs of the chair through which I was staring, as though they were bars through which I might see some glimpse of God. And the constant shrill cry of that word 'drunk' which I did not understand, but which I knew, with the intuition of childhood, was associated with madness, and disaster and death.

III

I would rather say that I did not see my mother that night, for she was not looking her best.

But I did see her, on my way back to bed. It was only for a moment, on the stairs.

She had been ill. I cannot remember what had been the matter, but it must have been serious, for she was the least hypochondriacal of women. She hated going to bed, and only stayed there under protest.

She was making her way down the staircase. One hand clutched the balustrade, the other held on to the arm of my brother Paul, who was entreating her to go back. She did not seem to be listening to him, nor to be aware of his presence. She was very pale; her hair, which was still long, hung loosely over her shoulders. She had thrown a dressing-gown over her night-dress. It was an old dressing-gown and a cheap night-dress. (I did not know this at the time; I thought that everything she had must be costly and beautiful. But the economies forced on us by our father's drunkenness had already begun.)

Slowly she came down the stairs, her eyes fixed on the open door of the dining-room. Through it I could see the bare table, and the candles guttering and a dim shape on the floor. Towards that shape she walked. It held everything she had loved – and continued to love, through every trial and degradation – until the day of her death.

She did not seem to see anything else. I ran to her. She

kissed me. She said, 'You should not have got out of bed.'
She was quite calm. Suddenly I felt at peace.

'You must go back to bed,' she said. 'Everything will be all
right.'

Because she had said it, I knew that it must be true. The
dim shape, which I could still see through the door, lost its
menace. The guttering candles were no longer like the eyes
of devils – they were just the kindly lights that had shone over
us on so many ordinary occasions. The night was robbed of
its darkness, God was in His heaven, and He had answered
my prayers.

My mother gently detached herself from my arms. She
told Paul that she had no further need of him. Step by step
in her cheap night-dress, she walked down the stairs.

Then she went into the dining-room, and shut the door.

IV

The following morning was bright and clear. It was early
in June, and normally I should have gone swimming, or
riding on my bicycle over the Devonshire hills. But today was
different. Tomorrow would be different, too; the whole of
life would be different.

I went to the window and pushed up the blind, half ex-
pecting to see a new landscape stretching before me. But no,
the prospect was the same. The garden was looking very
beautiful. Like many of the gardens of Torquay, where we
lived, it had a tropical air. There were palm trees on the terrace; against the old walls banks of fuchsias sprang six feet
high; far away, beyond the tennis court, you could see the
pale elegance of the eucalyptus, and through them the distant
glitter of the sea.

I dressed hurriedly and went down to breakfast. As I
passed the door of my mother's bedroom, which was next
to mine, I heard voices, and something that sounded like a
groan. All through the night those voices and those groans

Book One ⚜

had drifted through my sleep. It was frightening to think of what had gone on behind that door – what might still be going on.

My brothers were already down.

'Mother's having breakfast upstairs,' said Paul. 'So I'm going to pour out.'

'Is he up there?'

'Of course he's up there. I saw him. I took them up some tea.'

'How does he look?'

'Awful. All crumpled up, and groaning.'

'I hope he doesn't come down,' I said. 'Not like that.'

'He won't,' said Alan. 'The doctor said he mustn't.'

'Has the doctor been?'

'Yes. I went to fetch him. On my bike.' There was a certain pride in Alan's voice. 'And I helped to get him upstairs.'

'We all helped,' said Paul. 'Mother and me and Alan and the doctor. We had to push and pull. He said awful things all the time.'

'What sort of things?'

'You wouldn't understand,' observed Alan, with the superior experience of nine.

'And he was sick on the stairs,' chimed in Paul. 'Cook put ashes on it.'

I suddenly wanted to cry again. It was horrid having breakfast like this, without my mother. Horrid, with nobody to tell me to eat up my porridge, even if I didn't want to eat it. Why couldn't she come down? Why must she stay up there with that . . . that man?

'Is she coming down?'

'Yes. At ten. Then we're having a family conference.' Paul said the long words with grave importance. 'And she said that you mustn't tell anybody anything. She said speci-ally *you* mustn't.'

'Why specially me?'

'Because you went crying off to cook last night.'

'I saw you,' chimed in Alan. 'Going on like mad. And praying.'

I could think of no retort. It was all too true. I felt very unhappy, as though I had done my mother some harm, when all I was longing to do was to help. I got up from the table, and went out, leaving my porridge untouched.

'Ten o'clock,' cried my brother after me. 'In the billiards-room.'

V

The billiards-room was large and shabby and friendly. It was dominated by a huge moose's head, which hung over the mantelpiece. My father had bought it at a sale, but he used to tell people he had shot it in Alaska.

Most of the pictures had some sporting interest. The largest was an engraving of an international rugger match, in which my father had played; he used to point to his picture and say proudly 'That was me'. There were many photographs of groups, mostly of my brothers at school. As the years went by they were to be supplanted by groups of Oxford undergraduates, and in the end, of officers in the First World War. The last group hung on that wall showed myself in the centre, as President of the Oxford Union. Winston Churchill, who was then Home Secretary, was sitting by my side.

It should have been a happy room, with so much sunshine, and so much youth – indeed, till yesterday it *had* been happy. But now everything was different. My father's face – the face on the floor, with the wine-drenched moustache – seemed to be everywhere, in the mirrors, in the groups, even on the moose's head. Perhaps my mother felt this too, for when she came down, followed by my brothers, she said 'Let us go into the garden.'

She walked through the french windows and we followed

her to the end of the terrace. She sat down on a garden bench and we gathered round her.

I felt for her hand. 'Is he coming down?'

'No. Not until the doctor has been again.'

'Will he be . . .' I wanted to say 'safe', because I still thought of him as an animal, something dangerous that had escaped from a cage. But I did not like to show that I was afraid. So I changed it to 'Will he be all right?'

My mother said 'Yes.' But though she pressed my hand, to reassure me, I noticed that she did not meet my eyes.

Then she took command of the situation. She said: 'You must tell nobody about your father last night. Nobody.'

'But cook knows,' said Alan.

'And May and Anne,' added Paul, naming the other two maids.

'I have spoken to them. They won't say anything.'

'Shall I tell Miss Herridge?' I asked. Miss Herridge was my governess. She was a dear, but her piety was so intense that I wondered how she would react.

My mother thought for a moment. 'I think she will have to know. But I will tell her myself.'

'Whatever will she think?'

Alan scowled at me. 'What does it matter what she thinks?'

'It matters very much what _you_ think.' My mother spoke with special earnestness. 'And the most important thing is that you do not think unkindly of him.'

'Well,' sniffed Paul, 'we can't think very kindly of him.'

'But it was not him,' she said. 'It was _not_ your father.'

What did she mean? Had it been some stranger we had seen lying there, bloody and groaning?

'Not him?' echoed Alan.

'I mean,' she said, 'that he was not himself. Not his true self. He was ill.'

'But he was drunk,' protested Alan.

'Ssh!' She took his hand in hers. 'You mustn't say that.'

9

'But he was . . .' 'But he was . . .' Paul and I joined our voices.

'No. *No.* It was not that. At least . . .' My mother paused. She did not seem to know what to say. She looked very unhappy and very ill. 'His heart,' she murmured. 'It's his heart. He says so. And the doctor . . . the doctor told me it was a disease.' She repeated it again, as though to reassure herself. 'The doctor told me it was a disease.'

We looked at each other, without speaking. We did not understand. A disease? But that was quite a nice thing to have. You came out in spots, and your mother sent for the doctor, and you stayed in bed, and did not go to school. Everybody was kind to you, and gave you sweets and flowers. Surely that was not the same as drinking and drinking, till you fell down and cut yourself and shouted terrible things?

Paul broke the silence. 'Can we tell people that he has a disease?'

'No. You must not tell people anything.'

'But, Mother, supposing . . .'

'There is no supposing about it.' Her voice, usually so sweet and gentle, sounded almost sharp. 'I will not have you telling anybody. And I will not have you thinking unkindly of him.'

We stayed silent. I stared up into the branches of the greater guelder-rose, which I knew by the name of the snowball tree. It was in full bloom, and I remember thinking how strange it was to see snowballs against the skies of June. Up and down they danced in the breeze, light and cool, as though they were being tossed into the air by ghostly children hiding in the shadows.

How puzzling it was! My father had been drunk. But my mother, who could not tell a lie, said that he was not drunk; it was a disease. Yet we were not to tell anybody that he was ill, nor were we to think unkindly of him. This was perhaps the hardest thing of all, though 'unkindly' was not really the word that met the situation, at least, as far as I was concerned. It was not a question of unkindness, but of simple fear. I was still haunted by the illusion that he was an animal, escaped from its cage, who would come after me with claws and teeth, shining through that wet, black moustache.

There was the sound of a car coming down the drive.

'That will be the doctor,' said my mother.

She rose and left us to ourselves.

VI

A note about our story.

How can I remember so vividly and in such detail a conversation which took place so long ago?

There are two reasons, and they apply with equal force to subsequent conversations which will be recorded.

The first reason is because it is a conversation which I heard not once but a hundred times. It was my mother's theme throughout her life. 'It is not *him* . . . it is a disease.' I have heard that in spring, in summer, in autumn and in winter – in the morning, in the noon and the night. I heard it as a child, as an adolescent, as a young man, and as a man on the threshold of middle age. 'Not *him* . . . a disease.' In the face of insult, of humiliation, of bleak disaster, my mother was faithful to this theme. She never changed her tune. Never.

It has caused me to set a high standard for the other women who have come into my life . . . women with whom she has inevitably been compared.

And the other reason why I can write that conversation so easily, so accurately?

Because it was impressed on a youthful mind in a very high state of nervous tension.

From the age of six onwards this was my normal condition. Of course, I escaped from it while I was at school (though I learned to read between the lines of my mother's letters,

and was tormented by fears for her, as the years went on).
But on the whole it is true to say that the normal rhythms
of my life were set in three recurrent tempos – tension,
climax, pause – tension, climax, pause. In other words, he is
beginning, he is at his worst, he is recovering. But he was
never recovering; he was always recoiling, for another
spring.

When one's youth is lived at this perpetual state of nervous pressure, listening for the quality of the footstep outside a door – (is it firm or is it shaky?) – watching the grip of
fingers round a carving knife – (if the thumb sticks out at a
certain angle it means he is beginning again) – lying awake
at night, trying to interpret the groans coming from the
next room – (I learned to tell by their pitch and rhythm
whether they betokened remorse, anger, or a simple attack
of vomiting) – with all these signposts, the steps of youth
(and the very echo of those steps) are remembered all too
clearly.

Would that some of the conversations I shall record were
indeed fiction! But they are as near to fact as you are likely
to meet in this world.

Here is an illustration of the abnormality of my boyhood
existence.

About three years later I was walking home from school
with another boy. He put his arm through mine and said,
'Why don't you come home and have tea with us?'

'But do they know?' I asked.

'Know what?'

'Know that I'm coming? *Have you warned them?*'

There must have been some echo of fear in my voice for
I remember that we stopped walking, and that he was staring at me with a puzzled grin on his face.

'What a funny thing to say,' he said. 'Warned them of
what?'

'I wouldn't like to come unless you had warned them.'

When he saw he could not persuade me, he shrugged his

shoulders and went on his way whistling. I had lost another friend.

This is a simple picture but it tells a significant story. I was longing to go to tea with that boy, but 'home' to me was a place of guilty secrets. You must not ask people in to visit you casually; that would be courting disaster. They might come only after the most careful preparation and at certain very clearly defined periods, when 'he' was at the end of a bout, confined to bed – (but even then you had to be careful about the groans) – or a week later, when 'he' was up and about, shaky but sober, preparing to begin again.

The thought of strolling home, accompanied by a friend, without warning, was terrifying to me. To this day, the fear remains in all sorts of curious ways. I can never open the front door of my own house without a slight sinking in the stomach. The house is mine, the sun is shining, all is well, but as I turn the key in the lock my heart beats faster. 'He' may be waiting, on the other side of the door.

However, all this is anticipating. I made the digression in order that I should not be suspected of writing fiction when I am writing fact. Most of the conversations recorded in works of an autobiographical nature are somewhat tiresome, for they must obviously be largely imaginary. These are not.

We must retrace our steps.

It is June; I am six years old; and a tragedy has just befallen us.

The rest of this book will tell how, in our various ways, we rose to meet that tragedy.

Chapter Two ❧

My father stayed in bed for four more days.

This was the average period, as experience was to teach me. If we were to make a monthly chart of his life it would run something like this.

January 1st. Get out of bed. Two days of remorse, tears, and vows of penitence.

January 3rd. Normal for three days. Often gay and kind. In these three days he writes a great many letters, to show people how well he is, how firm his handwriting. He parades the town every morning, smartly dressed – his monocle brightly polished, his grey bowler hat at a rakish angle, a carnation in his buttonhole. 'What a charming man Mr Nichols is!' say the local inhabitants.

January 4th. He begins again. For five or six days he does not go to extremes; his stomach will not permit him. In this period he drinks only half a bottle of whisky a day; for him, a very moderate allowance. It does not prevent him from walking fairly steadily, nor from thinking – at least about business matters – with comparative sanity. During any of the days in this period he could probably pass a sobriety test.

There is only one change in him; he is turned into a devil in his personal relationships.

It is in this half-bottle-a-day stage that the bitterest things are said to my mother, the meanest tricks invented to torture her, the subtlest devices contrived to frighten all of us; or when we can no longer be frightened, to humiliate and perplex us. No human brain that I have ever encountered in fiction, and certainly none in life, was so regularly and so passionately employed, over so long a period, in the exclusive labour of making others unhappy. Greedily, like a vampire, he sucked energy and inspiration out of the misery and fear he had himself created.

January 9th. A week of total and hopeless drunkenness.*

He is drinking, at the least a full bottle of whisky a day, a good deal of strong ale, and frequent swigs of brandy. The effect of this stupendous consumption is heightened by the fact that he drinks on an empty stomach; for a week almost no food passes his lips.

This stage would probably be regarded by the average onlooker as the worst; it was certainly the most dramatic. This was the week in which to listen for the sound of his body crashing to the ground in some distant room; this was the week of blood on his forehead, where he had hit himself against the wardrobe, or on his hands, where he had smashed a window-pane, because he thought he was choking and wanted air.

This was the week when the servants usually gave notice.

'Never in my life, madam, have I heard such language.'

'I am very sorry, May,' my mother would say. 'But he was not himself.'

'That may be, madam, but then there's Anne. You can't expect *her* to want to stay, with such goings on. Half naked, he was, the other night, lying in the hall.'

*In future accounts of my father's various conditions of drunkenness as our story unfolds I have used the word 'delirium' to characterize the fourth and final stage of the cycle. However, this should not be taken to indicate the classic condition of *delirium tremens*.

(*Delirium tremens*, as generally understood by the medical profession, has much in common with an epileptic seizure; the limbs are violently convulsed. The brain is totally deranged, and even if the victim is a man of comparatively frail physique he is endowed with a superhuman strength, so that at least three other men are needed to control him. My father seldom reached this extremity; it was as though the spirit possessing him, at the last moment, withdrew. But he came so close to it that I shall allow the description 'delirium' to stand.)

'I did not know that he had got out of bed.'

'Yes, madam. When you were in the garden.'

'I will not go into the garden when he is like that.' (Yet the garden was her last retreat – I have seen her lift her arms to the branches with a gesture which reminded me of a hunted soul, seeking sanctuary.) 'I will not go into the garden. It shall not happen again.'

Cook sniffed. 'I'm sorry, madam. And we're all very sorry for *you* too. But we can't stay.'

And so my mother would be dismissed, again and again, by her own servants. Throughout these humiliations, she kept her dignity and her sweetness. No servant we ever had was rude to my mother. I believe they would have stayed if they could have borne it, merely to help her, because they loved her. But they could not bear it. The horror of our home was too much for them.

This problem of the servants reminds me of one of my father's endearing little ways. Whenever a servant had left us on his account, he would take the first opportunity of parading the town and mentioning the fact, lightly and gaily, in conversation. Something like this:

Mrs X: 'And how is Mrs Nichols?'

My father: 'Very well indeed, full of energy, a wonderful woman!' A slight pause. And then, as though he had suddenly remembered it . . . 'Of course, she's a little worried now. The servant problem!'

Mrs X: 'No? *Again?*'

My father: 'I'm afraid so. My wife, bless her heart, doesn't seem to have the gift of keeping servants. Now, if only you could tell her *your* secret!'

Mrs X (delighted by the flattery): 'Oh, but there's no secret. Just a little management. That's all.'

My father (bravely): 'Well, let's hope we shall be luckier this time. I don't complain for *myself*. I don't mind what I eat! It's just for *her* sake.'

16

He smiles, and lifts his hat, and as he bids her goodbye he looks at her with a gallantry that is not lost on her. 'Such a charming man,' she thinks, as she resumes her walk. 'Mrs Nichols, too, quite a dear, and certainly a *lady*. But what a pity she's such a bad manager. Now if only *I* had the running of that house . . .'

My father walks on his way, preening himself. He has done his good deed for the day; he has sowed his seed of poison. Soon it will be twelve o'clock, and he will go into the Queen's for his first double whisky. The barmaid is a friend of his; she will be sympathetic when she hears the news about the cook.

At home my mother, for the hundredth time, is instructing some new girl in the mysteries of our kitchen.

'I hope you will be happy here,' says my mother when she has finished.

'I'm *sure* I shall, madam,' says the girl with a beaming smile. For she feels that she would do anything for so kind and gentle a lady.

But she has not yet met my father.

II

We digressed at January 9th, the fourth stage of my father's bouts.

I suggested that an outsider would find this the worst stage of all. It was not so with us, for somewhere about the middle of it my father could usually be lured to bed. There he stayed, and as long as he was given a bottle of whisky to keep by his side, he was not likely to move.

Then we could relax. By contrast, we were happy. Meals became almost sane; we could actually indulge in ordinary conversation, without fearing that it would be broken by an angry snarl, telling us that we had unwittingly touched on some forbidden subject. My mother could console herself in the garden; I could do some work. It was as though he had gone away, or were dead, and our lives were lit by a wintry sunlight.

But he had not gone away, and he was not dead. Even while he lay up there, temporarily immobilized, his personality was so dark and dominating that he seemed to fill the house, his spirit seeping through the closed door of the bedroom and drifting down, hovering around us.

The thought of that bedroom, and the fact that my mother nightly opened the door of it, and went in to him, became a torture to me. From the very beginning it seemed to me a Chamber of Horrors.

During the bed-ridden periods, I would usually be deputed, at meal-times, to take him up something on a tray. A little soup, or a slice of chicken, or some fruit. It was a waste of time, for he never touched anything. But my mother insisted that the tray went up. She had taken him for better, for worse, in sickness or in health. She would carry out her obligations not only in the spirit but to the letter.

So I would go upstairs with the tray. It was right that I should do so; it was not a job for the servants, who would have been revolted by the scene behind the door, and I was glad to take this small burden from my mother, who had been waiting on him all day and would be with him all night.

But how I hated that little task!

I would stand outside the door, the tray in my hands, summoning up courage to go in. Downstairs I could hear the slow tick of the grandfather clock in the hall, and perhaps the low murmur of my mother's voice, talking to my brothers. There was a big skylight over the stairs, and the rain lamented on it and the wind rattled it mournfully. It always seemed to be a night of wind and rain, as I stood outside the door. But it was not for those sounds that I would listen but for the sounds from inside the bedroom. Not till I was nearly twelve did I become immune to the animal groans and the strangled retchings.

Then I pushed open the door. There he was before me, in the big double bed. It was a four-poster, hung with heavy curtains of green tapestry, and sometimes his arms and legs would be tangled in them, so that I would have to pull them straight. Usually he lay on his back, staring with a sort of cloudy rage at the ceiling. He was in his night-dress, which clearly revealed the rolls of fat in which his body had become encased. His mouth was always wide open and whatever sounds came from it were ugly, whether it was a maudlin 'thank you, my dear, thank you' – or merely a queer, rather frightening 'Ah! Ah! Ah!' as if he were dying. Once, I remember, he just stared at me and muttered 'Bloody, bloody, bloody.' That struck me as rather funny, for I was older at the time . . . nearly thirteen. I went downstairs laughing. But when I told my mother why, she looked very unhappy, and I was afraid she was going to cry.

III

I mentioned above, in this chart of my father's existence, that in his fourth stage, when he was bed-ridden, it was our custom to give him whisky, in order that he should not stagger out on to the streets to get it himself. This method of dealing with the problem caused my mother endless searchings of the heart. She reluctantly accepted it after years of experience had taught her that if she did *not* give it to him, he would get it somehow, even if he had to crawl to it on his belly. Indeed, it was only after a particularly grotesque scene, where he had been caught just outside the drive, on all fours, crawling through the mud in the direction of the town, that she decided it was better to put a bottle within easy reach, so that he could drink himself to a standstill.

This technique was not employed in the first three stages – only in stage four, when all hope of 'pulling himself together' had vanished. Even so, as I said before, my mother never ceased to reproach herself.

And to her own reproaches my father, incredible as it may sound, joined his.

At the end of every bout, when groans and sobs of remorse were echoing from the bedroom, my mother would come downstairs, and we would go through some such dialogue as this:

'I feel so wicked,' she said, 'ever having given him anything.'

'But, Mother, you only did it when he'd got to the stage where he'd fall down in the street.'

'I know. But *he* says I'm encouraging him.'

'Of all the filthy things . . .'

'Please don't say that. He's sorry this morning.'

'How very kind of him, after giving us hell for three weeks!'

Then the pain on my mother's face would make me repent my bitterness. I would try to be moderate.

'I'm sorry. But he should realize that you only do it as a last resort, to save him from disgrace, to keep him at home.'

'He doesn't seem to see it that way.'

'But you never do it till the very end. There's never a drop of drink to be seen in this house, normally. You never touch anything, nor do we. There's nothing stronger than lemonade on the sideboard. You even go round to see where he's hiding it, and take it away. But when he's got to the stage where he's a raving lunatic, clinging on to the furniture, you simply can't let him go out. You've got to give it to him. Unless you want a scandal.'

'Anything would be better than that.'

'So you always say.'

'I would endure *anything*, rather than public disgrace. Don't you agree?'

I would say 'yes', just to please her, but I did not agree. A day was to come when I longed for his public disgrace; I would lie in bed, dreaming hot and angry dreams in which I

20

testified against him in a court of law, when I strolled past his cell and spat in his face.

And I am not, as a rule, a good hater.

However, we have looked too far into the future. We must go back to that day in June . . . the first stage of the first bout.

Chapter Three ❧

'He is coming down this morning,' said my mother.

We had just finished breakfast, the three of us – Paul, Alan and myself.

We exchanged glances, but we did not speak.

'I want you to be as nice to him as you possibly can. He has been very ill, and he feels very sorry about everything.'

Still we did not speak.

Then she added a plea which she only used on the rarest occasions. 'For *my* sake?'

So Paul said, 'Of course, Mother.' And Alan said the same. I do not remember what I said, but it must have been satisfactory, for my mother left us with a smile.

A few minutes later my brothers had gone off to day school. I felt lonely and apprehensive; I dreaded seeing my father again. It was not so much fear which beset me as a queer sort of social embarrassment. That is an odd emotion for a child of six, and obviously, at that age, I·should not so have described it. But that is what it was – the kind of diffidence that besets one if somebody has committed an appalling social gaffe and one has to pretend not to notice it.

What should I say? Just 'Hullo'? Or would he speak first? And where would we meet? Supposing I saw him at the top of the stairs would I have to wait for him to come down, and then say something? Would we shake hands? Or might it be better to meet in the garden, to run past and shout 'Hullo' and not stop? Or would that be 'unkind'? It was all very difficult, and I knew that whatever happened, my cheeks would burn and I should want to sink into the earth.

As I was pondering these things, the problem was momentarily solved by the arrival of Miss Herridge, my governess.

II

Miss Herridge was a saint.

It is significant that so sweet and honest a word as 'saint' should have an ironic echo, in these days. 'She was a saint?' you ask. 'You mean a prude? A prig?'

I mean nothing of the sort. I mean 'saint' in its purest form, to indicate one who is very close to God. It would be an understatement to say that she had one foot in heaven and the other on earth; she had both feet in heaven, and only reluctantly did she walk the ways of men. Even then, she walked as a saint, seeing in all earthly things a heavenly meaning. To her, the flowers in the hedgerows were petals that had drifted through the golden gates, to give us a faint foretaste of the eternal gardens awaiting us; and the stars at night were pin-pricks in a vault behind which blazed an infinite rapture of light.

Not that she was vague, or even 'pi', in the schoolboy sense. She was an excellent governess, neat, methodical and well-read; and she had a store of unusual knowledge, not usually shared by nursery-governesses. She was a first-class botanist; she encouraged me to form collections of wild-flowers, and mount them neatly in albums, with their English and Latin names. I have the albums to this day. Some of the gold lingers on the petals of the celandines and the anemones still hold a hint of blue, like a sky that is dimly remembered, once so radiant, but now clouded over by the years.

She could cook, too, delicious cakes and sweets; and she had a pretty taste in music; she swept aside the ancient bundles of Sidney Smith which represented my father's taste and led me to the simpler sonatas of Mozart. Sometimes when I was playing them on one of our two 'grand' pianos, which were always out of tune, I would watch her face and think she was like the angel in the window over our pew at church. Then I would play a wrong note, and in justice to Miss Herridge it must be recorded that the angel immediately stepped out of its frame and threatened to rap me on the knuckles.

III

But she was the wrong person to help with regard to my father; she lived in too rarefied an atmosphere. Before her eyes there flowed the eternal blood of the wounds of Christ, so how could she be greatly affected by the blood that my father had shed on the dining-room carpet?

'Miss Herridge,' I said, as we sat down at the big table in the morning-room, 'Daddy's coming down today.'

Miss Herridge beamed. Radiance flowed from her as from some powerful internal battery.

'I'm *oh* so glad!' she cried. This was her favourite form of articulation. The accent was on the 'oh', which was pitched sweet and high; the 'so' was very short, a sibilant with barely a hint of a vowel, and the 'glad', or whatever the adjective might be, was slightly tremulous. Thus: 'OH s'glad! She put her whole heart into the phrase; and since her heart was pure gold, the phrase itself always sounded like a paean of adoration, even when the adjective was itself uncomplimentary.

Sometimes she would look at my hands and say 'Oh so dirty!' But though she made me wash them, the phrase 'Oh so dirty!' always had that curious, incongruous quality of ecstasy; it was as though she saw through the dirt on my hands to the rich soil of the earth in which I had been dabbling; and the earth was the Lord's and all that in it is, and her heart could not contain the joy of worship.

I find it impossible in this book to avoid the temptation

*John Nichols and Pauline Shalders at the time of their engagement, with their
respective signatures. The graphologist might find confirmatory evidence in these
signatures of the clash between a delicate and a brutal personality.*

My *mother as a girl, and as an old lady. She had been ravaged by suffering, and hid her face from the camera.*

Uncle George, one of our few 'respectable' relations, whose sole contribution to the tragedy was to burst into tears.

The author as a schoolboy, when his profile aroused unorthodox emotional reactions, including the gift of a copy of The Picture of Dorian Gray. (*See Chapter 7.*)

Children of Promise (L to R) Alan, myself and Paul, shortly before my father took the first steps that led to fifty years of tragedy.

Backgrounds for murder, 1: Cleave Court, Torquay, the chief of our 'Haunted Houses', and the milieu for most of the action in this book. Cleave Court was the scene of my first two youthful attempts at murder. (The tennis court – see pages 116–118 – was on the lower lawn and is out of the picture.)

Backgrounds for murder, 2: the cottage at Glatton in Huntingdonshire, of which I wrote in Down the Garden Path, *and the study looking on to the garden.*

My brother Alan during his brief career in the Gordon Highlanders.

My brother Paul as an Oxford undergraduate.

Paul after our father's death.

to digress. For a moment we must leave Miss Herridge and myself sitting at the morning-room table; I want to tell a story which will show her as she really was.

It was nearly thirty years later. Miss Herridge was then over sixty and I was thirty-five. I was very happy, for I was busily engaged in writing the Chronicles of Allways* which were as nearly a labour of love as any literary work can be. In one of these books – *A Village in a Valley* – I had drawn freely on my memories of Miss Herridge, whom I called Miss Hazlitt; she drifted constantly through the story; and though the adventures I ascribed to her were fictitious, they were true in essence; they were *her*, reacting as she would have done had she walked down the paths which I invented for her.

One day, when I was actually writing an imaginary conversation with 'Miss Hazlitt' I received a letter from Miss Herridge. As I read it my heart sank. She had come to London; she was in Charing Cross hospital; she had had an operation, but another was necessary. Such was her news, though it was given almost as an 'aside', among long passages praising the love of her Saviour and the overwhelming mercy of God.

I hurried down to see her; it was a bright day in early spring and on the way I bought a bunch of the simple flowers that she loved so well, primroses and violets, grape hyacinths and 'glory of the snow'. It was a very grand shop where I bought the bunch, and the attendant wanted to wrap it in cellophane, but I deterred her; Miss Herridge would not like to see this sparkling mask of sophistication over the flowers of spring.

The hospital was a gaunt building in one of the noisiest and most hideous parts of London; as a hospital it was doubtless efficient but the architect seemed to have designed it with the deliberate intention of enhancing in stone the

* Published under the titles *Down the Garden Path, A Thatched Roof* and *A Village in a Valley*.

horror of pain. A very bright nurse received me, and whisked me up in a lift to the third floor. For a moment she left me while she conferred with the matron, and I remember sniffing the bunch of flowers and thinking how strange it was that the faint fragrance of a few primroses could triumph over the reek of disinfectant.

The nurse came back. 'This way!'

She led me to a ward reserved for serious cases; several beds were screened, and from behind them came deep-drawn sighs. One or two pale faces turned as I came in.

'Here she is!' cried the nurse, leading me to the corner of the room. And then, in a louder voice . . . 'A visitor to see you!'

Before me lay an old lady, her eyes half closed, her breath coming slowly and painfully. I had never seen her like this before; her hair was white and her face and throat were wrinkled. I turned to the nurse. 'I think there is some mistake,' I whispered. 'I came to see Miss Herridge.'

As I said the words, the old lady's eyes opened, and she breathed my name.

I stepped forward. I knew it was her, and yet some part of my mind rejected the knowledge . . . that part of the mind which is ceaselessly engaged, till the last moment of life, in thrusting pain and age and death into the background. 'To this must we all come,' mocked the brain, 'all youth and bloom and gaiety must shrivel into this.' We need not pursue a theme which has inspired some of the world's greatest poetry. Besides, a moment later Miss Herridge seemed to come back, with a flood of memories, in the single phrase:

'I'm *oh* so glad!'

Thirty years were swept away by that phrase; once again I was the boy and she was the teacher, and as I handed her the flowers I remembered the many other bunches I had picked for her, in the hedgerows of the Devonshire lanes, white violets and ragged robin, periwinkle and celandine and foxglove. And I felt the old nervousness which I used to feel when I had forgotten their Latin names.

We talked of the past, which need not concern us. The only reason I tell this story is for its ending. As I rose to go I said: 'I am so terribly sorry to hear your news. After all you have been through – to have to endure it all again. It's too bad.'

'Oh but *no*!' And now her voice was firm and clear. 'No!' Slowly she struggled to sit up; I tried to help her, but she thrust me aside. I know she had something she felt very important to tell me.

'You must not say that,' she said. 'It was not too bad at all. When I came round, after the operation, and when they told me that I should have to have another one, I was so *thankful*.'

'Thankful?'

'But *oh* so thankful!' she repeated. For a moment I seemed to hear again the faint echo of the thrush that used to sing so sweetly in her throat. 'You see . . .' and here she put her hand on mine . . . 'it meant that He was testing me again.'

She looked into my eyes, and smiled. That smile, and the light in her eyes, were as near to heaven as I am ever likely to see. She had not many teeth, her eyes were dim, round her shoulders was a shabby shawl, and through the window behind her was silhouetted the hideous outline of Charing Cross. But these things counted for nothing; she was a beautiful woman, and the place where she lay was very near to Paradise.

IV

'I'm oh so glad,' cried Miss Herridge.

We are back again in the morning-room, thirty years before; I have just announced that my father is going to come down again.

'Have you seen him yet?' she asked.

'No.' A pause. 'What will he look like, Miss Herridge?'

'Why – he will look splendid!'

I pondered the word. Splendid. It did not sound convincing. I had never thought that my father looked 'splendid'. He was a huge man, and in his youth he had been extremely good-looking, but now . . .

'And you will be very nice to him, won't you?'

I bent over my lesson. Miss Herridge must have taken this as a gesture of assent, for she said no more. But as I tried to read, I could not help thinking how odd it was that everybody kept harping on the importance of being 'nice'; it seemed at variance with all that I had been taught of life; of crime and punishment, of sin and retribution.

We were doing a simplified version of Greene's *Short History of the English People*; and certainly, in this book, the historian gave no suggestion that 'niceness' should be the reward of sin. Although he wrote with the decorum of an eminent Victorian, his pages were stained with blood, and it was not the blood of the virtuous. But my father had also been bloody, covered with blood, and yet his reward was that we were to be specially 'nice'.

I could not grasp it. I looked up from the book, and I said:

'But, Miss Herridge, he has been wicked.'

For a moment she did not understand. Then a shadow of pain crossed her face.

'Hasn't he been wicked?' I repeated, hoping that the shadow meant that she would agree.

The shadow passed as quickly as it had come. For the word 'wicked' to Miss Herridge – as indeed all words – was automatically translated into heavenly terms. Were we not *all* wicked, in the eyes of God? And was it therefore possible for us to assess the degrees of our corruption? When one of us committed some extra sin, as my father had done, should we not take it solely as an occasion to offer redoubled praise to God, whose Infinite Mercy was the only reason why we were not *all* bundled straightway into the Pit?

Such was her argument, and such were her words.

'But we are *all* miserable sinners,' she cried – and she rejoiced so fervently in her protestation that the words 'miserable sinners' sounded like a phrase of music. 'All of us,' she echoed, 'miserable sinners. And we can only be saved through Him.'

The capital H escaped me. Or perhaps I allocated it incorrectly. Him with a capital H meant my father. Henceforth and for ever more. But when Miss Herridge spoke of Him or He she had no thought of any but Jesus.

'Only through His blood,' she went on, 'the blood of the Lamb.'

That word 'blood' again. It gave me small comfort. Blood, to a child of six, is a frightening thing; to me it was particularly frightening for reasons which I need not reiterate. I could not direct my brain into these mystical channels with the fragile assistance of the word 'Lamb', for Lamb carried with it an irreverent but inescapable odour of mint sauce. Blood . . . my father's face . . . Him . . . the Lamb . . . the words went round and round in my head but they made little sense. All I knew was that they all seemed to be red words, with blood on them. And I said:

'Will he have washed away the blood?'

Miss Herridge stared at me. What had the child said? What was going on in my mind? Then she too understood; she forgot her angels and her archangels, she emerged from the darkness of her heavenly illumination into the clarity of the sunlight that filtered through the lace-curtains on to my face. She took me in her arms and said:

'You look very pale. You must not be frightened. Of course he will have washed away the blood. And you must promise to be very nice to him.'

V

The lesson was over; Miss Herridge had departed; my mother had gone out. And still the ordeal of meeting my father lay before me.

I had a sensation of panic; I wanted to run away. Where was he? Had he come downstairs? I tiptoed from the morning-room and stood in the hall, listening. Never had the house seemed so quiet; there was such an empty background that the ticking of the grandfather clock was like the beat of a lonely drum; I could hear the fall of a rose petal in the silver bowl by the window.

I tried to be brave. This was absurd; I was acting like a baby. Was I not six? 'Be nice, behave as if nothing has happened.'

It might be a good thing to play the piano; he might come in while I was playing, and that would be a way of passing off the first awkward moments.

I crossed the hall, my footsteps echoing over the polished floor, and opened the door of the drawing-room. The air seemed chill, for the blinds were half-drawn, but He was not there. So far, so good.

Stealthily I went to the piano. Stealthily because I felt that I was being watched, that he was hiding somewhere, to pounce upon me. I sat down, closed my eyes, and took a deep breath.

Courage!

I breathed in the fragrance of the drawing-room. The sense of smell is of all senses the most evocative; to this day I can recapture the elusive essence of that long, lofty room, so crowded with furniture and bibelots and yet so restful and tranquil. It was all brown and beige and ivory, and from its many tables and side-pieces arose a multitude of faint perfumes, from the china bowl of pot-pourri on the stool by one of the fireplaces, from the pot of dried lavender that always stood on the mantelpiece, from the collection of sandalwood boxes that one of my uncles had brought from India, and from the flowers themselves . . . the almost painful sweetness of roses in silver bowls, and the sharp tang of rose-geranium, which my mother always used to place by a screen near the door, so that we could pinch a leaf as we came in.

There were other scents too, even more delicate, such as the ghost of the perfume that lingered in a tiny crystal phial on a table near the window. My mother told me that it had once contained attar of roses, of which a single drop had cost a whole pound. That may or may not be true, but she believed it, and so did I. I would sniff it, in awe, thinking of the acres of blooming roses that must have been cut to yield one drop of this magic nectar.

The fragrance of the drawing-room assailed me, enveloped me.

I began to play.

A small boy, very frightened, with brown curly hair and bare, scratchy knees. Playing the piano, in a frenzied effort to ward off an evil spirit.

And still He did not come.

VI

The scene is etched so clearly that I can still hear the tinkle of the old piano, and see the picture that hung by my side, as though it were before me today.

This picture has a special significance in our story.

It was three pictures in one frame, and it was entitled 'The River'. The first tableau depicted the stream at its source. It was morning; the sky was blue and innocent; lambs frisked in the foreground. The second showed a broad river running through a valley. It was afternoon; and though the sky was still blue its tone was more adult, and a warning cloud gathered over the hill. The lambs had grown into sheep,

31

and had been pushed into the background. In the third picture it was night and the river was nearing its end; in the distance, under the light of a crooked moon, shone the sea. Lambs and sheep had been left far behind; somewhere in the background loomed a factory chimney.

In the margin the artist responsible for this triptych had inscribed the predictably appropriate lines:

> Men may come and men may go
> But I go on for ever.

In those days I thought it was a beautiful work of art. So did my father. Since I had some talent for improvisation it was his habit when we had guests to lift the picture from the wall, stand it against the music-rest, and desire me to improvise on the three phases of the river. It sounds embarrassing and no doubt it was – the infant prodigy contemplating the picture, lifting his fingers, and then 'interpreting', for the space of some twenty minutes. And no doubt the 'interpretation' itself erred on the side of the obvious; simple arpeggios for the source (with a few trills for the lambs), a broad-flowing waltz for the river (with an occasional lapse into the minor for the warning cloud) and a succession of funereal chords, in common time, for the final phase. But it impressed the guests, and I admit that I enjoyed it. All too much, I fear, for the habit of improvisation is like the addiction to a drug; it gives one exquisite moments but it is sterile. If the streets of hell are paved with good intentions, the streets of heaven are paved with improvisations; indeed, that is one of the chief reasons for wishing to go there, that we may have the chance of hearing, down some silver corridor, the music that drifted through a window of Majorca, long ago, when Chopin was playing and when the rain was on the roof – music that poured out carelessly, to mingle with the sigh of the wind and the wave, and be lost. Lost? Maybe . . . maybe not. I try to be on the side of the 'maybe nots', hoping against hope that beauty is

32

eternal, that the discords cancel out, that only the sweet sequences remain.

VII

Today I could not play.

My fingers would not work; each time I struck a chord I lifted my hands sharply off the keyboard, drowning the echo with the soft pedal, and listened for his step.

Then I heard it, slow and heavy on the stairs, coming down, step by step, nearer and nearer. I wanted to fly but I was trapped. What could I do?

There was a pencil on the table by my side. I seized it and began to draw pictures on a piece of manuscript paper that lay on the music-rest. I drew feverishly, as though my life depended on it, flowers, animals, faces. I could draw no better than the average child, and it must have been a strange hotchpotch, particularly as my fingers were shaking so violently that I could hardly hold the pencil.

The steps drew nearer; he had reached the bottom of the staircase; he was crossing the hall, the door creaked open; there was a pause. Still I drew, quickly, quickly. The steps came on again.

He was behind me now.

'Hullo.'

I did not turn round. I felt very faint and rigid, and my throat seemed to have sand in it.

'Drawing?'

'Yes.'

'What are you drawing?'

'Things.'

'What sort of things?'

He came closer. He was leaning over me. I became more rigid than ever. He was still the animal, the big, wounded animal who had lain on the floor, and had tried to get up,

33

and follow me. Stiff and still I stayed, staring at the paper before me.

Then I put my hand, quite suddenly, over the paper. Over the 'things'. Even as I did so, I thought to myself . . . 'You are not being kind. Mother told you to be kind. It is not kind to put your hand over the paper like this.'

I could not help it; I did not want him to come into the world of my dreams.

There was a sigh behind me. I have often been haunted by that sigh.

I slid away my hand, in remorse. There – he could look at the drawings now. He was very unhappy. I could tell that.

Across the paper fell a shadow.

I stared at it. It was the shadow of a rose.

The shadow was trembling. I watched it quivering on the paper. Maybe I am reading into my thoughts at this moment emotions which were then too mature for me, but I do not think so. The scene is so very clear, lit with the cruel clarity of remembered grief – the sunlight on the paper, the blurred drawings, the trembling shadow.

Slowly I turned round. I met my father's eyes. His lips moved, but he did not speak. Moved again. In a strange, hoarse voice he said:

'I thought you might like this.'

He laid on my drawings a yellow rose.

It was at its most exquisite moment. It was of the ancient race of Gloire de Dijon, carved from sunlit ivory.

There it lay, with the dew on it. I could think of nothing to say. I stared at the rose, and when I turned, he had gone.

To this day I can never see a Gloire de Dijon rose without also seeing, falling across it, my father's shadow.

Here we must be allowed another digression – though it is a digression in time rather than in mood.

In later life I was to gain some reputation as a gardener, as a maker of gardens and a writer on gardens. But I have never been able to grow a rose. Though this, of course, is an overstatement, in essence it is factual. Wherever my paths have led, whatever the soil or the climate, the roses in my gardens have faltered and faded and died. If one had been a bungling amateur, if this had happened only once or twice, there would be no point in mentioning it. But I was not a bungling amateur; I had learned in the hard school of experience; in most aspects of gardening I could hold my own with the experts, and, on occasions, where they had failed.

But never with roses. When a great firm of nurserymen asked if they might give my name to a rose I was naturally flattered. By all means. What more charming memorial could a man desire? The 'Beverley Nichols Rose' was still-born. It was hailed with a flourish of trumpets, but it with-ered on the stem. The men who had perfected it – and they were not 'bungling amateurs' – were bewildered. What had happened? Could I suggest where they had gone wrong?

Yes I could. But my explanation would hardly have been accepted by the Royal Horticultural Society, for it would not have been concerned with questions of botanical muta-tions or horticultural expertise. It would have been a psy-chic explanation implying a spiritual malaise, transmitted from father to son, from stem to leaf, from leaf to flower, poison generating poison through every root and branch – shadow following shadow.

In my gardening library there are, as far as I am aware, no suggestions by the experts as to how the practical gardener should cope with such phenomena.

In my present garden, which will surely be the last that I make in this world, there are very few roses, and those that survive are pale and sullen. Even in the sunlight they seem to shrink into the shadow, and when I walk towards them, they look away.

Chapter Four ✤

A month later he had begun again.

We did not know it at the time. By many subterfuges and manœuvres my mother managed to conceal the fact from us; there were no open breakdowns, no collapse in public. True, he was periodically 'ill' and confined to bed, and his 'heart' was giving him a great deal of trouble, which was why he stormed and swore and behaved so strangely. Again, there were a number of mysterious accidents; he had fallen on the terrace, 'because the gardener had been so foolish as to leave the roller at the top of the steps', and he had hit his head on a beam in the coach-house. And he was always cutting himself when he shaved.

Neither I nor my brothers as yet connected these symptoms with drunkenness; they were afflictions which might beset any man; indeed, we felt sorrow for him rather than anger, for my mother took every fresh mishap as an opportunity to entreat us to be 'nice' to him.

For the rest of her life – over thirty years – this was her golden rule.

'A soft answer turneth away wrath.' I heard her say that a hundred times. I violently disagreed with this philosophy; and I believe it to have been a fatal one with regard to my father. In his case, as I was later to prove on more than one melodramatic occasion, there was only one effective form of treatment – physical violence. He had to be hurt, and hurt very hard. He had to be made to suffer great physical pain, and the day was to come when I was to be the instrument of his suffering. I have not the smallest regret about this, although I write as one who believes that cruelty is the worst of all sins – indeed, that cruelty is the essence of all sin, that

36

it lies at the core of every crime in the calendar. But the infliction of physical pain in such circumstances was not cruelty, it was a form of self-defence, and, in its way, a last desperate attempt to cure him when all other therapies had failed.

But my mother, on whom by far the greatest share of the burden fell, would have none of this. He must not be hurt, mentally or physically, by word or by deed. That was her philosophy and nothing would turn her from it.

Let us trace her origins and try to guess the secret of her bravery and her strength.

Pauline Lillian Zoe Shalders came into the world on October 22nd, 1866. She was the youngest child born to my grandfather, Alfred Shalders, a fairly prosperous woollen merchant whose business was at Bradford. His other children I remember as Aunt Kate and Uncle Julian.

The family tree is of all forms of literary vegetation the most tedious and I do not propose to explore it at much length. Nor need we concern ourselves with theories of heredity. However, two stories about my grandparents have perhaps enough interest to receive a moment's attention.

Long after my grandfather was dead my mother gave me his gardening notebook. I myself was deep in the enchantment of making a garden at the time, and I was particularly excited by the problem of growing winter flowers out of doors. I wanted not only snowdrops, winter jasmine and the few brave plants that are to be found in most gardens during the dark months; I wanted rarer things, bolder and more brightly coloured.

This search for winter flowers became something of an obsession. It was difficult to gratify, and few other people seemed to share it, but little by little my list grew longer – a hint in some old book, a discovery in some out-of-the-way catalogue. A week or so later a muddy parcel would arrive at the cottage and out I would rush in the wind and the rain and the sleet to find a place where the precious object might have some hope of survival. Often, I must admit, it did not survive, for I was madly optimistic, trying to make semi-tropical plants grow in the sullen clay of Huntingdonshire. But there were surprising successes.

Then my mother gave me my grandfather's notebook. One night, when I opened it, and turned its yellowing pages under the lamp-light, I found, to my excitement, that he had shared my passion, had followed the same paths in the same spirit, and had made the same discoveries . . . indeed, many more. Sixty years before, this man whom I had never seen had bent over the soil of his Yorkshire garden, even colder and more windswept than my own, tending the same plants, which in those days must have been of exceptional rarity, and going to his study, when darkness fell, to write their names and their progress in a handwriting which was almost identical with my own.

The flowers seemed to bloom again, drifting across the faded pages where he had so lovingly inscribed them; winter-sweet and winter honeysuckle, iris stylosa, that pierces the armour of the snow with swords of blue. He had the flowers that linger late, like the winter daffodils and the Kaffir lilies, that always remind me, when I see them in the ragged beds of December, of the last guests in a deserted ballroom; and he had the flowers that arrive long before the dawn of the year, particularly the winter aconite, whose golden blossoms flower undaunted even under a sheet of ice, like a Victorian posy poised in a glass case. All these he had and many more. Side by side with the chronicle of their progress he had scribbled remarks like – 'I love a good fight' – (apropos of his attempt to save a sick camellia) . . . and 'The sunlight made the wintersweet so fragrant that a few foolish bees appeared from nowhere and buzzed round in a dazed way. I hope they come to no harm.'

My grandfather's love of winter flowers caused his death; he died of pneumonia because he insisted, against his doctor's orders, in making a tour of his beloved flowers on a freezing day in February.

There are worse ways of dying.

The mention of death reminds me that I can tell, more briefly, an episode which illustrates the character of my grandmother. One day, when she was a little over sixty, she felt ill and went to bed. The doctor diagnosed heart disease and ordered complete rest. However, she could never rest; she adored parties and people and laughter and music; and within a very short time her bedroom was transformed into a sort of salon – a daring innovation in Victorian Yorkshire. It was on the fifth day, when she was receiving guests, that somebody told her a story that she found especially amusing. The silver teapot was in her hand, the tray was spread on the lace coverlet. She laughed and laughed, trying vainly to pour out tea. She cried, 'Oh dear, I know I shall die laughing.' Then the teapot fell from her hand, a cup was broken, a stain crept over the coverlet, and she was dead.

There are worse ways than that, too, of going to meet one's Maker.

From two such people my mother was born; they were lovers of life, they were gay, and the sun shone on them.

My father's family was of a very different stock . . . twisted, harsh and thorny. *His* father was also a drunkard, though a restrained one, and he had more than a touch of sadism, for he beat his sons unmercifully, with a 'ground ash stick', whatever that may be. He called himself a 'gentleman farmer'; there is little evidence of his gentility and though his farms prospered, he was so mean that he never sent my father to a public school nor a university – an omission of which we were constantly reminded. 'I never had *your* advantages,' my father would storm at us.

The only member of the Nichols family with whom we had any contact was my father's brother George. But our meetings were few and far between, partly because my father hated him – and even more vehemently hated George's wife Blanche, whom he insanely suggested was 'probably riddled with syphilis'. The reason why there was so little contact was because both Uncle George and Aunt Blanche were congenital misers, who lived in constant dread that they might be called to our assistance, and thereby involved in some small expenditure.

These words may sound unseemly to those few persons who still live to remember Mr and Mrs George Nichols of 8, The Avenue, Clifton, Bristol. George Nichols, to them, was an upright, hard-working, God-fearing man; his wife a pattern of domestic rectitude. They were esteemed by their friends and respected by their servants; and though they were perhaps a little old-fashioned, they did nobody any harm. Why, then, this bitterness, when they are no longer here to defend themselves? For one reason, which to me is compelling. Uncle George and Aunt Blanche were quite literally the only relatives to whom my mother could turn in her hour of need; there was nobody else at all; and when, in desperation, she called for their help, they ran away. No, that is not quite true. They did, in fact, come down from Bristol to stay for one night, but when Uncle George saw my father stretched on the floor, all he did was to burst into tears. After which he sent Aunt Blanche upstairs to lie down, observing to my mother that 'Blanche is not *used* to such painful scenes'. They departed by the first train on the following morning, and Uncle George's final words were that he might be obliged to change their third class tickets to first class, because poor Blanche was 'greatly upset'. From that day onwards they washed their hands of our tragedy, never referred to it, never even offered a word of sympathy. From time to time, in an effort to shame them into some sort of activity, I would write to ensure that they were fully aware of what was happening at the Haunted House. Every letter was ignored except one, in which Uncle George reproved me for writing in so 'unfilial' a manner. 'It is a pity,' he added, 'that you cannot find some nice girl, who would direct your mind to higher things. Your Aunt and I are great believers in the married state.'

Such words, addressed to myself, to whom 'the married state' meant only my mother's torture, were cruelly insulting.

By comparison with my father, Uncle George, it need hardly be said, was a model of all the virtues and indeed, in his earlier years, he had qualities which I would like to think were hereditary. Thus, he had a genuine love of wild flowers, which – like myself when young – he mounted in albums, with meticulous neatness. He had an endearing affection for cats, with whom he carried on conversations which showed a subtle comprehension of the feline character. But little by little, under Blanche's corrupting influence, his nature narrowed and his interests shrivelled, so that in the end he was as fanatically miserly as herself. Some of the examples of his parsimony are so bizarre that sometimes I feel that I must have invented him. But I did not invent the letter which arrived on my ninth birthday informing me that since I and my brothers were now 'nearly grown up' there would be no more birthday presents. A card would be enough. The card in question was a twopenny one; the price had been marked in pencil on the back, and Uncle George had not quite succeeded in rubbing it out. Nor am I inventing the many curious incidents which occurred when, as a schoolboy, I went to stay with him in Bristol. When I arrived – (he had generously gone to the expense of sending a postcard giving details of the cheapest bus) – both Uncle George and Aunt Blanche were on their knees in the hall, cutting up newspapers which they were laying across the carpet into the drawing-room. They adjured me to keep to the centre of the newspapers lest my small feet should stray on to the carpet and ruffle up the pile. It was not an exciting visit; the only entertainment they offered was an occasional visit to a free museum. And yet I enjoyed it, even though our evenings were spent sitting bolt upright in the drawing-room, with our feet firmly planted on the newspapers, listening to Uncle George shouting denunciations of 'the modern world'. As he shouted and as we listened, we sipped hot water, into which Aunt Blanche had squeezed the juice of half a lemon. 'God's wine' was how Uncle George described it, at the top of his voice. And though it was not very nice I sipped it gratefully, reflecting that at least it would not give any of us *delirium tremens*.

A last comment on this weird couple, for misers have always interested me. Once a year Uncle George and Aunt Blanche made a trip to London. They could well have afforded to take a suite at Claridges, though I did not learn this till many years later. Instead, they lodged at a dreary pension near Paddington Station, where they obtained 'special terms', after a great deal of tedious correspondence with the manageress. Among the 'special terms' was an understanding that they could have their luncheon in the form of a packet of sandwiches which they would be allowed to consume outside the premises. This they did. Clutching their sandwiches, they queued for a bus to Piccadilly. Here they arrived at ten minutes to twelve precisely, and entered a cinema. Apparently, if one enters a cinema before noon, one gets in for half price. Having entered, they proceeded to nibble their sandwiches, and sip the contents of their thermos flasks, and when the programme had run its course three hours later they remained firmly in their seats and saw it all through again.

After Uncle George died, Aunt Blanche lived on for another twenty years, in apparently increasing impecuniosity. Among my varied literary output is an annual Calendar in praise of cats, of which she sometimes bought a copy. One year the price of the calendar was raised from five shillings to six and she wrote to inform me that this sum was beyond her means, so she would be obliged if I would send her a free copy. When I replied that I would be happy to do so, she wrote again to suggest that perhaps I would let her have a dozen copies every year, so that she could send them to her friends instead of Christmas cards. And it would be thoughtful if I would stamp them in advance. Her letters were written on scraps of used paper such as the backs of old envelopes and they were plentifully interlarded with patriotic sentiments and references to 'Our beloved Queen'. They frequently contained malicious little digs about my own activities.

Thus, if I went for a lecture tour in America, there would always be a letter awaiting my return to the effect that I had been 'gadding about' and should try to 'settle down'. *She* could not afford such luxuries, *she* had to stay at home and 'keep the home fires burning', and *she* did not know what she would do if the price of coal went up any more. One of her favourite phrases was 'We were brought into this World to Work'. In spite of this façade of poverty she was careful to foster the belief that one day – ('When I have gone to my Maker') – there would be benefits in store, dropping hints about her lawyers – ('with whom you will be dealing one day').

I am afraid that I seldom Rallied Round. From time to time, as the years rolled on, I would go down to my mother's grave at Long Ashton, to say a prayer and to lay a bunch of flowers, and since this was only a few miles from Bristol I felt obliged to call in to see Aunt Blanche. But these calls became increasingly depressing. Heavier and heavier grew the scent of moth-balls in the narrow corridors, thicker and thicker gathered the dust-sheets over the Hepplewhite chairs and the Sheraton settees. She had collected many beautiful objects around her; Uncle George had been a shrewd judge of values, and night after night, as he sipped his hot water – ('God's wine') – he had been in the habit of sitting at his desk with a copy of *The Financial Times* on one side and a copy of *The Connoisseur* on the other, comparing the merits of a Chippendale commode with a holding of

43

Imperial Chemicals, in terms of capital appreciation. 'I wonder what will happen to these things when I have gone to my Maker,' Aunt Blanche used to sigh, casting a beady eye upon me. The implication was so obvious, and so subtly insulting, that this was usually my exit cue. There was a charming Chippendale mirror in her hall which would have gone well in my music-room, but if it were ever to have come my way I should always have seen in it the reflection of her face. It is not a face with which I would care to live, for it is one of the masters that glimmered, however dimly, in the dark halls of the Haunted House.

When Aunt Blanche died she left the world huddled up in coarse patched sheets, mended and remended till they looked like a patchwork. Upstairs, smothered in moth-balls, were collections of the finest Irish linen, stuffed into an exquisite bow-fronted wardrobe which, I gather, is now in the Victoria and Albert Museum.

Her Will was attested at £175,000, which, even in these days, is not to be sneezed at.

There is only one other member of the Nichols family who need be mentioned, and he was probably the least unattractive. This was my Uncle Arthur, who died of tertiary syphilis in Australia at the age of seventy. He was my grandfather's favourite son, and caused a minor sensation, in the nineties, by hiring the Gaiety Theatre for one afternoon in order to play Hamlet. He had never appeared before on any stage, even in amateur theatricals, and his interpretation of the role was, to say the least of it, unorthodox. The gallery was soon denuded of pennies, and on the following morning the critics excelled themselves in a concerted burst of vituperation. 'Hamlet without the Prince' was the verdict of *The Times*, though even *The Times* was obliged to pay tribute to his looks. Like many of the Nichols family he had the *beauté de diable*. He sounds rather fun to me, but my father did not think so. The Hamlet venture cost my grandfather

44

five hundred pounds and it was only one of many similar escapades which helped to lighten the family purse.

Sometimes when I have been reading Dostoevsky I have regretted that the great novelist never had the opportunity to study my father's family. However I fear that he would have thought them distinctly overdrawn.

II

Near the beginning of this book is a picture of my mother as a girl. She is dressed for her first ball, and I think she looks beautiful. The dress was of pale yellow silk over dark brown velvet, and the ruffles at the wrists were of old Irish lace.

'Before we set out for a ball we used to sit very close to the fire,' she once told me. 'Kate and I, by the fire, roasting our cheeks. First one side and then the other, so that we should have a pretty colour when we arrived.'

That was the greatest height of vanity to which she ever attained; during the latter years of her life she hardly bothered even to look in a mirror. She looked *at* mirrors, yes, to see that their surface was clean and sparkling, and on some occasions to make sure that there were no specks of blood on them. But of the slowly changing reflection of herself, the counterpart that stood before the silver surface, always a little slighter, wearier, more lined with care, she saw nothing.

The picture you have seen, which shows her ten years before I was born, is my favourite likeness, because it tells me that she had a few years of spring and sunshine. She had once been happy. That is what I can tell myself. She had laughed and danced and flirted, and been kissed in conservatories, and fluttered her fan. Long, long before I was born.

Once, I heard her mention, with a mingling of apology and defiance, that seventeen men had proposed to her. The apology was due to her innate diffidence in attributing to herself any sort of merit; the defiance was a desperate

45

reaction to a sneer of my father's to the effect that he had saved her from being an old maid. 'And one of the men,' she added with a sigh, 'is now a millionaire.'

I would like you to learn to know my mother very well, so I have printed a picture of her when she was old, that you may compare it with her picture when she was young. Time ravaged her mercilessly; beauty fled; but those who loved her will tell you that even to the last they never saw a smile so gentle nor heard a voice which sang with so sweet a music.

Let us pay a visit to her dressing-table, which may tell us more about her.

III

A Proust might have written a cycle of novels round her dressing-table. For many years it was the only feminine province which I was able to explore. Ours was a house of men, standing in a world almost entirely composed of men. That is why mother, apart from being an object of love was also an object of awe, simply because she was a woman.

I used to tiptoe to her bedroom when the house was quiet, and wander round this dressing-table, fascinated by its mysteries. Later, when life showed me glimpses of other dressing-tables, lavishly spread for beautiful women who were luxurious and pampered, I would remember the few humble vanities of my mother, and a feeling almost of hatred for these rich women would come to me; I wanted to sweep their scents and creams and powders to the floor.

The principal object on the table was a silver powder-box. Her initials, P.L.Z.N., were engraved on the lid, and it was always kept brightly polished. I used to take it to the window, to see how prettily the trees and the sky were reflected. The wall outside was covered with roses, and if you tilted the box you saw the image of roses sparkling on the surface, yellow dots against the silver, with a filagree of leaves as delicately chased as on some ancient Chinese snuff-box.

The powder in the box was pure white, scented with violets. Had my mother been a vain woman she would have realized that this was the very last powder she should have used, for she had a high complexion. But powder, to her, was simply something that one put on after washing. She applied it in the most rough and ready way, dipping the puff into the box, shutting her eyes, screwing up her face and dabbing vaguely at her nose. The result was not, cosmetically speaking, desirable, but to me, as a small boy, it was an act which never lost its power to fascinate.

The powder-box was the sole tribute my mother paid to Venus. But no – I am forgetting. There were other things, but they were not the sort of things which would arouse much interest in the patrons of Elizabeth Arden. There was usually, for instance, a bottle of some sort of scent – but such a pathetically small bottle and always of the cheapest lavender water or eau-de-Cologne. When I was older I was able to give her perfumes of a different sort, chosen merely because they were so luxurious and so feminine. Her reaction to these gifts was unexpected; it was in direct proportion to their cost.

'It's very beautiful. But what *must* it have cost?'

'Never mind. Open it and see.'

'Oh no. I don't think I want to open it.'

'But that's what it's for.'

'Not yet. Perhaps at Christmas. Just a few drops. I'm sure it was terribly expensive?'

Then she would look at me, with an expression of the liveliest curiosity. At first I misread that expression; I wanted to be told that the money had not been wasted. So I would say that the bottle had only cost a few shillings. But then a shadow of disappointment would cross her face. So next time I told her the truth.

47

'Five pounds? Oh no, you *shouldn't* waste your money like that!'

But there was delight in her voice.

'It's absurd. It must be about a shilling a drop!'

'Do open it and smell it.'

'Oh *no*. Not until some special occasion. I want to keep it and enjoy it.' Then she would take it over to the mantelpiece and put it there for all the world to see.

'It makes me feel wicked,' she would say, with a crinkled smile. 'Five pounds!'

This thrill which she felt when she realized the cost of the presents I sometimes gave her was the natural reaction of one whose whole life had been a long struggle to make both ends meet. While my father was drinking away the pounds she was desperately engaged in trying to save the shillings, washing and ironing, weeding and hoeing, mending, darning, cleaning. A house of our size demanded at least four servants and two gardeners. She ran it, towards the end, with one maid and an odd man.

That was why she felt this irrational pleasure in the thought that she was being given something that was costly and charmingly useless. She must indeed have been even more deeply moved than I suspected, for one of the very few occasions on which I ever saw her crying was when she found that my father had fallen against her dressing-table, and had smashed one of these precious bottles. She went down on her knees, and dabbed a handkerchief on the carpet. 'It is so unkind of him,' she kept saying to herself. 'So very unkind.'

IV

The dressing-table was of Victorian walnut, large and solid and what my mother always described as 'good'. That word 'good' was a relic of her Yorkshire upbringing. It had no connection with beauty or elegance, it was simply a tribute to

48

sound workmanship. Sometimes I would say to her that a particular piece of furniture was hideous, and that we ought to get rid of it.

'It *is* ugly,' she would agree. 'But it is *good*.' And there the argument always ended.

The dressing-table, though 'good', was not ugly. Perhaps I am prejudiced, for as I said before, it was my earliest introduction to the temple of feminine mysteries. Some of these were so strange that they were positively frightening.

I shall never forget the day on which I discovered that she dyed her hair. One afternoon, passing her bedroom, I looked in and observed with a shock that the bottom drawer of the dressing-table was open. I had been reading the story of Pandora's box, which was still vividly in my imagination. I stopped and stared, waiting. The house was very still, and everybody was in the garden. I stood there, watching for a black claw to creep over the edge, or the tip of a crooked wing, or the glitter of a serpent's fangs. Then I said to myself: 'I am ten. One is not frightened at the age of ten. I shall go and look.' I walked into the room, paused a moment, and then went straight to the drawer.

Needless to say, none of Pandora's creatures were present. But something else was present – a little black bottle, a stained tooth-brush, and a saucer. What new mystery was this? It did not take me long to learn; it was all written on the label.

My dismay was profound, and it was due to the feeling that I had discovered my mother in an act that was not strictly honest. My trust in her was unlimited. She was synonymous with truth. But now, it seemed, she 'touched up' – to use the scandalized expression of that period. For a moment I tried to persuade myself that perhaps it was my father who used the dye. However, that was obviously wishful thinking, for he was grey round the temples, whereas her hair was unflecked.

It was only many years afterwards that I saw this small

artifice on my mother's part as one of the countless sacrifices she made to my father's whims. It was for him that she did it because, as he sweetly remarked, he didn't see why she wanted to go about 'looking like an old hag'.

She stopped dyeing her hair when she was fifty. It was a great day for her when my father gave his gracious permission. She came downstairs jubilant, and threw the bottle into the waste paper basket. 'I always hated it,' she said. 'It made me feel so silly ... "getting myself up".'

Her hair was prettier from that time onwards, a delicate grey with a soft bloom that hinted, in the sunlight, of the rich chestnut which it had been when she was a girl.

V

Is she coming to life?

Not as clearly as I could wish; the picture is still dim. Maybe that is because she was nearly always effacing herself, hiding in the background.

Although she may evade us, in a physical sense, it is easier to give a picture of her mind. For this, let us visit her bookshelf. Her reading was largely confined to two types of book, and they each had their special function, the one as an antidote, the other as a nepenthe. The antidote was typified by Emily Brontë's *Wuthering Heights*; she read it at least twice a year, and always it comforted her. It was as though the dark storms that swept over its pages had some power to obliterate the storms that swept through her own house, as though the gigantic figure of Heathcliffe stepped between her and the figure of my father, giving a mask of fiction, fierce but noble, to the sordid face of fact. Often she would say at the end of some ugly scene, when at last my father had been lured to bed, when the crisis was over and we could sit by the fire and relax ... 'That was just like *Wuthering Heights.*'

The other class of book which consoled her was typified

by Mrs Gaskell's *Cranford*. To her it was a pot-pourri that never cloyed, in which the scent of each flower became more beloved with the years. In the lanes of Cranford she roamed at ease; the wild roses were always there to welcome her, and they were the sweeter because they could not be plucked; and the doors of the Cranford ladies were always open to her, Miss Matty, Miss Pole and the Honourable Mrs Jamieson; and often, in imagination, she entered those doors and wandered through the tall, dim rooms – a ghost of the twentieth century, seeking sanctuary. I think that they would have made her welcome, the ladies of Cranford, and I know one of them at least who would have shaken her bonnet very energetically at my father, had she known the truth.

Antidote and nepenthe; the angry chord of the dominant and the melting resolution of the major key – these were my mother's refuges, and there was little else between. It was either *Macbeth* or *Pippa Passes*.

But no – that, alas, is untrue. For my mother never shared Pippa's pleasant conviction that 'God's in his heaven, all's right with the world'. Since this last consolation was denied her, her own tragedy was all the more grievous.

VI

She was not a religious woman. Her philosophy was simple. If you had asked her to define it she would have replied: 'To go to bed every night knowing that I have not done anything unkind, or hurt anybody or told a lie, and that I have helped others as much as I can.' As she always did go to bed with this knowledge, and often with the additional consolation that by sheer pluck, mental and physical, she had surmounted situations which would have sent most women screaming out of the house in terror, she ought to have felt fairly happy about her position in the after-world. But she did not.

She longed to believe; she went to church; she prayed;

but the idea that Jesus Christ had died to save her, and that one day she would meet Him face to face, was something that she simply could not grasp.

'A *person*?' she once said to me. 'Meeting a *person*?' And she shook her head.

Nevertheless, we went regularly to church, and when my elder brother took holy orders my mother was delighted, maybe because it gave an odour of sanctity to a family which was poisoned at its source.

Those church-goings . . . what an unutterably different world they conjure up! My father, needless to say, never went, though he was very insistent that we should do so. We had to walk over a mile across steep hills; in spite of this we were nearly always the first to arrive, for my mother was of all women the most punctual. Service was at eleven, but at ten she was already 'dressed', and chafing to be off. On the silver card tray that stood near the front door there were always two slices of dry bread, which she used to eat just before setting off, 'to prevent rumbling noises during the sermon'. Every time she ate the bread her face used to crinkle up with a smile, and I used to hope that the bread would not work, and that there *would* be rumbling noises, because I knew then that my mother would be trying not to laugh, and that was much nicer than seeing her trying not to cry.

A sense of humour is not an entirely desirable asset for those who seek, through the Church of England, the rewards of religious conviction. My mother kept hers, through thick and thin. I will give one slight example, though, in doing so, I am obliged to anticipate. In our next chapter we shall provide a simple guide – a sort of Horror Chart – to the various stages of degradation through which the acute dipsomaniac must pass in his descent to his self-created inferno. For the moment, it is enough to mention that in my father's case the last stages of his bouts were always marked by days and nights of vomiting, and the task of holding the basin for him was one which my mother always insisted on taking into her own hands. But one night she was so exhausted that she asked me to come into the bedroom. I went in, and I held the basin. By then I should have been immune to sights like this, but sickness has always been very disgusting to me. Apparently I held the basin at arm's length, with one hand, and with an expression of unutterable haughtiness on my face. Suddenly, above the groans and the retchings, I heard another sound. It was my mother laughing, helplessly. She lay in a chair, shaking from head to foot. 'Oh, if you could see yourself,' she cried, 'if you could only see yourself! You look so outraged!' And then I laughed too, and the groans and the laughter mingled in that long room of shadows and secrets.

This sense of the ridiculous was constantly stepping in between my mother and – I will not say God – but the Christian interpretation of Him. She loved the language of the Psalms, but she found it difficult to avoid smiling when one of our neighbours, appropriately named Miss Faithful, was in the pew behind her singing:

'All my bones are out of joint: my heart is like wax; it is melted in the midst of my bowels. My strength is dried up like a potsherd; and my tongue cleaveth to my jaws.'

For Miss Faithful was not only a hypochondriac but another dipsomaniac, and this confession sounded exactly like her conversation at one of her own tea-parties.

All the same, Church did us good. Even if we did not really 'believe', it was nice to be, even for an hour, among people who were clean and kind; it was nice to hear words that were sweet and gentle, and to be quite sure that, as long as we were in these hallowed precincts, the air would not be split by obscenities. There was a touch of envy about my own feelings; I used to look over the nodding, feather hats, and the bald heads, and say to myself 'It's easy for *you* to be good; you're going home to an ordinary luncheon, and perhaps there'll be wine on the table, instead of whisky on the top of the bedroom cupboard. You'll be able to discuss the sermon without wondering if every word you say may be taken as an offence. Yes – it's easy for *you*!'

In spite of this, Church did us good. We had taken a plunge into the normal world. When we came out, and lingered in the porch with a bow here, and a word there, I realized that my mother was reassuring herself as to our social position. 'Lady X was so charming.' She would not have been charming if she had 'known'. And the Admiral had walked with us up part of the hill. He would not have done that if he had 'known'.

Perhaps if my mother had enjoyed even a few months of peace, she might have stepped out of the evil spell which my father cast around her, she might have acquired some of the spirit of Mary to offset the spirit of Martha, and a very browbeaten Martha, at that. This respite was never granted to her.

VII

My mother was afraid of death.

It was not till near the end that this melancholy realization forced itself upon me.

For the last seven years of her life – she died at the age of seventy-three – she was very frail. During this period, in a hundred ways which she fondly imagined were unnoticed, she showed that she was frightened.

For instance, she was always pathetically eager to hear of the exploits of women older than herself. 'Eighty seems to be nothing nowadays,' she would say. 'Here is a story in the paper of a woman of eighty who still goes to dances.' And she would draw herself up in her chair, and stare into the fire, and I knew she was whispering to herself: 'Ten years more – I need not worry, yet!'

I soon learned the significance of her interest in the very old, and since it seemed to give her comfort, I used to collect every available scrap of evidence about her seniors. If an octogenarian went skating in Canada, or a nonagenarian mounted a bicycle in Mexico, I was always the first with the news. My prize catch was when I discovered that my own housekeeper's grandmother was 101, and still walked three miles a day.

'So in thirty years' time, Mother darling, you will probably be wheeling me in a bath-chair.'

She laughed, and shook her head. But the story helped. She was always anxious to learn more about this remarkable old woman. 'Are you *sure* she's 101? It seems too extraordinary. And walks three miles *every* day?'

'But that's no reason why you should do the same,' I would warn her.

A mile, indeed, was more than enough for her. Her blood pressure had mounted to dangerous heights, even on a strict diet, and even with the aid of constant sedatives it was seldom below 230. Her heart was like a bomb that might explode at any moment. For seven years she lived and slept with death. In any normal household she might, even at the age of seventy, have been pulled round; even a month's relief might have wrought a physical miracle, but this relief she never gained.

It was hard for an old lady.

The doctors used to say to her, with becoming gravity, 'At all costs you must avoid any nervous strain.' Since her entire life was spent in an atmosphere of Lyceum melodrama my mother may be forgiven if sometimes, on hearing this advice, she permitted herself an ironic smile.

On one occasion the smile broadened into irrepressible laughter. It happened like this. I had taken her to visit a famous Harley Street specialist – not because there was much hope that he could do anything – but because it comforted her to feel that she was getting the best advice. This man – his name was Sir Charles Purves-Stewart – delivered himself of a learned lecture, and at the end of it he summed up: 'Now remember, apart from diet, there are two vital things: no nervous strain, and no *stooping*.'

55

It was then that my mother caught my eye and began to laugh. And I laughed with her. Sir Charles must have thought we were mad, but we could not stop – the irony of the situation was too acute. For on the previous day, there had occurred a scene at home which was exceptionally macabre, even judged by our family's standards.

This was what had happened.

My mother and father were then living with my brother Paul in his vicarage in Cambridge Square. The house was too large for their means, and the problem of my father was made more difficult by the fact that it was necessary not only to 'keep up appearances' but to preserve the illusion of ecclesiastical sanctity. This my mother usually contrived to do, but there were moments when it was impossible; and it was one of these moments which we had remembered when Sir Charles said, 'No nervous strain, *and no stooping.*'

My brother was bringing the bishop home to tea. He was a new bishop and it was important that he should receive a good impression. So she had seen that the drawing-room was looking its prettiest, with fresh flowers and sparkling silver and a cheerful fire of logs. All this was done by three o'clock and since she had not been out all day she decided to go for a walk in the park. She went up to see that my father was 'safe'; yes, he lay in a stupor, a bottle of whisky by his side. Then she gave some last instructions to the new housemaid, put on her hat and went out.

See her as she walks down the square, rather bent, and with steps that are inclined to drag, keeping close to the gaunt iron railings, and pausing longer than seems necessary – as old ladies will – at the traffic lights. It is very close to the park, and soon she is inside, and has crossed a stretch of grass and is sitting down under her favourite tree. From here she can see the daffodils dancing down the side of Park Lane, and she thinks of the gardens she has had in the past – the Red House in Suffolk – Long Ashton near Bristol – Cleave Court in Devonshire – all so beautiful, and all so far away. It would be nice to have a garden, but her gardening days are over; she should be thankful she is so near the park.

Yes, she thinks, she has much to be thankful for. Her home, her sons, above all the fact that all these years she has avoided the public scandal that might have come so easily. When the bishop arrives for tea this afternoon he will never guess that he is stepping into a mad house. It will never occur to him to think that upstairs is a man who had just been snarling obscenities at her.

This is a book of digressions; every note I hear evokes a host of echoes, ringing down infinite corridors of memory. I cannot close my ears to those echoes. One of them is suggested by the word 'obscenities'. So let us leave my mother for a moment, as she sits there in the park, and attempt the difficult task of explaining what we mean by this ugly word.

VIII

As a rule 'bad language' does not much affect me; the monotonous f-s of the men in the forces seem no more deplorable than the 'too terribles' of another branch of society; they are a form of convention, that has lost its power to shock.

But my father had a brand of obscenity peculiar to himself; it was not so much the words that he used as the images which those words suggested, and these images, among which my mother was always prominent, were constantly projected before her in speech whose very rhythm was evil. If he had been a medieval sorcerer he would certainly have gained a wide reputation as a weaver of foul and poisonous spells; I have never known any man who could take the simple words of the gutter and shape them into a pattern so unspeakably disgusting.

I once heard him say something to my mother which, years later, I tried to repeat to one of the few friends who shared our secret. He had accused me of exaggerating. 'Very well,' I retorted. 'I'll give you one example. As you know, he never said these things to her in front of his sons; he knew that we shouldn't have been able to control ourselves. So his choicest phrases were always kept until the door was shut. We had to guess what had been going on. But this was an occasion when the door had been left open. And I heard him say . . .'

'Well?'

'It was a sentence of eight words.'

'But what *was* it?'

I made an effort. Then I gave it up. 'I'm sorry. I can't tell you.'

'What do you mean?'

'I literally cannot get it out. It's too filthy.' I saw a look of bewilderment in his eyes. 'I know this sounds idiotic. It probably is. If it were just a question of ordinary swearing I'd be perfectly happy to take on a drunken bargee for an hour, and beat him hands down. This is different. If I were to say it aloud, I should be sick.'

It was this sort of language which was waiting, as her normal reward, for the old lady whom we left in the park.

But something else was waiting, too.

IX

She rose to her feet. It was half past four and she must be getting home. There was nothing much to do, but she wanted to make sure that the fire was all right, and that the new parlour-maid had not done anything foolish.

Back over the stretch of grass, a last look at the daffodils, along the dreary stretch of railings. She turns into the square, fumbles in her bag for the key, opens the door, and then . . .

A white-faced maid is hurrying down the stairs, carrying a suitcase.

'Anne, where are you going?'

She starts and pauses.

'I . . . I'm going away.'

My mother feels a twitch of pain round her heart. But she does not show it. She shuts the door quietly.

'Going away?'

'I can't stay in this house. Mr Nichols . . .'

Another twitch of pain. What has he done now?

Automatically from years of habit, she says: 'Mr Nichols is ill.'

'Madam – look!'

The maid points to a dark corner behind the stairs leading down to the basement. Then my mother sees. He is lying there, on his face. That would not be so bad, but he happens to be naked. And the back-view of a naked man of seventy, enormously fat, rolling and groaning in the dust, is not exactly the sort of sight with which one wishes to confront a bishop on whom it is necessary to make 'a good impression'.

'We must get him upstairs at once.'

'Oh, madam, I *couldn't*.'

My mother looks at her. She is only eighteen; there are proprieties to be observed.

'I will put something over him.'

She hurries to the cloak-room to fetch a towel. She almost runs. No question now, of being an exhausted old lady with a weak heart. She fetches the towel, and a sponge, and an old overcoat. As she returns, the front door bangs. It is the maid who banged it – she has fled. Since it is cook's afternoon out, my mother is alone with the monster.

Now you will see why my mother, on the following day, found it impossible not to laugh when that great specialist pronounced the verdict: 'Above all, no *nervous strain and no stooping*.' For this was an occasion on which there was quite a lot of nervous strain. As for stooping . . . she had not only to stoop, but to pull and to tug, to take hold of his fat hairy arms and try to raise him into some position where he might be induced to listen to reason. Mercifully my brother came in early, before the bishop arrived, and between them they managed to drive him back upstairs.

That little episode probably took another year off my mother's life; soon afterwards, she took a turn for the worse. Her blood pressure soared, she would be very white one moment and very flushed the next. For the first time in her life her handwriting, which had been so pretty, and had always reminded me of the curling tendrils of young vines, became shaky and jagged.

Yet the more tenuous her hold on life, the more desperately she clung to it. She was afraid of death; it was her only fear, but it was a major one.

And so, we continued our empty search for a 'cure'.

X

One of our medical expeditions is etched on my memory with a special poignancy. I had taken her to see my own doctor – a brilliant young Swiss who was making a name for himself in the West End. He lived off Curzon Street in the heart of that part of Mayfair which Michael Arlen had made his province. His consulting-room was very gay with chairs of chromium plate and scarlet leather; there was a Tcheliatchev over the fireplace, and a signed picture of the latest star of the ballet on his desk . . . in those days it was probably Rabiouchinska.

Into this temple of fashionable science I led my mother – a figure from another age, bent and tired and very timid. It was the sight of her timidity which seemed to take me by the heart and give it a sickening squeeze; she sat there, blinking towards the light, trying to pinch her mouth up into a smile, pretending to be at ease, though the way in which she kept pressing her hands together showed her true feelings. She caught my eye, as I was watching those hands, and thereafter they were still.

She gave the familiar recital of symptoms, and he replied with the equally familiar recital of methods of treatment. He was a good doctor and an honest one and he held out no magic talisman of health. As she listened to him, and realized that he had nothing new to tell her, that he could weave no wizard's spell, the light slowly faded from her face. That is a phrase popular in fiction; this time it really happened; it was as though she had been in sunlight and was now in shadow. 'This is Beverley's own doctor,' she had said to herself, 'and Beverley is of the new world; somehow he will see to it that I am made well.' But now, she was alone again, with her weary body and her fluttering heart, and there was no escape.

She rose to leave. She was very polite; the pinched mouth managed to smile, and she waved her hand vaguely at the Tcheliatchev and murmured that she thought it was charming – which I am sure she did not. I thought the interview was over, and that somehow or other she would manage to cover up her disappointment, in order to avoid giving me any embarrassment. But this time she failed.

'Goodbye, doctor.'

I moved forward to open the door. My mother stayed still. Then she said four words in a voice that was all the more tragic because she tried to make it light and gay, four words which were nothing in themselves but from her were an evidence of great spiritual agony. She said:

'Nobody wants to die.'

She said them looking towards me, but I did not dare to meet her eyes. I had nothing to give her in response to the appeal that was in them. Nothing but my own grief to add to hers.

'Nobody wants to die.'

She did not say it again, but it seemed to echo round the room. It was mid-October – her 'favourite time of the year' –

and the sunlight that poured through the windows had already that faint tinge of silver in which the winter frosts are foreshadowed. Soon the leaves would be turning, and there would be bonfires in distant gardens, and blue smoke curling through the bare branches. Where would she be, by then? There would be the bitter smell of chrysanthemums, and the dead leaves would race down the lanes, and underneath, cold and green and sharp, the first spears of the snowdrops. Where would she be? It was unthinkable that these things could go on without her – that there should be night and darkness, the fall and flame of the leaf, the rise and swell of the sea; it was unthinkable that the great play should go on when she was not there to see it. She never *had* seen it, properly . . . always the drama of life had been blurred for her, made misty by a curtain of unshed tears, interrupted by shouts and curses, robbed of any unity except the design which she had arbitrarily imposed upon it by the integrity of her own spirit. Could she not see it, just once, in peace? Could she not have just one year, to watch it alone without the black shadow by her side? I felt that if she could have had this blessing, she would have gone to death not as one who steps down into a grey tomb but as one who opens the door of a secret garden.

If . . . if . . . if . . .

In a dream, I saw her standing by a tall window, looking out with me upon the world. It was winter; the whole year before us. And I would say to her . . . 'We will watch this prospect of snow and sleeping branches, see it unfold and blossom, flame and fade, and become again a naked pattern. But when we have seen it we shall know that it *is* a pattern, that it is a design, and a beautiful design, of which you are a part. We shall have stood by this high window and watched the clouds pile up and scatter, join hands and vanish, and it will not have been just a lunatic dance of vapours, it will have been a *design* – a message, if you will, that we shall have read together. You have had no chance to read that message, but I, who sprang from your body, have learnt it – or try to believe that I have learnt it. And most anxiously I wish to impart it to you, to prove to you that there is an eternal truth in Christ's words about the sparrows falling to the ground – a truth with a million gentle variations. For equally, no petal drifts on the wind unheeded, no raindrop falls at random, and even the cry of the loneliest seagull is noted on some scroll that passes human comprehension.

I might have told her all this, and telling her, have convinced her – as I believe, against belief – that the sombre figure of my father was necessary in a design that was etched by a hand of infinite love. But I never had the chance. Always, life intervened; my own hot passions blurred the picture; the melody was interrupted by a sob, or the ring of a telephone, or a drunken hiccough.

Yet, the melody remains. She did not hear it then. Maybe she hears it now.

Chapter Five ✢

Nearly a year has passed since the scene in the dining-room.

During the whole of this period my father has been drinking, but my mother has managed to conceal the fact; then there comes an afternoon when she can do so no longer. I must describe what happened, for it forms the first lesson in the Child's Guide to Dipsomania.

In later pages we shall not be obliged to dwell at such length on this melancholy subject; we shall take it for granted, like a fixed backcloth in a play, brooding continually over the actors passing beneath it. But before the reader can visualize this backcloth, and carry it in his head, he must be acquainted with the elementary outlines of dipsomania in practice, as seen through the eyes of a boy.

My mother and I had been to the 'Electric Palace', one of the early houses of the silent movies. In case you should have the idea that she was a gloomy woman, made morbid by the shadow hanging over her, it may be recorded that she had been consumed with secret laughter during most of the picture, which was a luridly sentimental tale of mother love. The mother had been played by an ageing ingenue with blue-white hair, who sat in a rocking-chair wrapped up in shawls, bestowing kisses upon her strapping cowboy sons, who referred to her as 'Li'l old lady' and 'the best sweetheart man ever had'. This was too much for my mother, who put her hand on my knee and whispered, 'Please *promise* me that you will never go on like that when I am an old lady.' Of course I promised, but I was a little shocked by my mother's irreverence, because I had rather seen myself as a cowboy, chasing bandits away from old ladies in rocking-chairs.

The picture over, we set out for home. It was a long walk, through noisy streets, up a steep hill that overlooked the harbour, and then along the winding, leafy roads of the 'villa district' in which our house was situated. As we drew nearer home my mother became less talkative, and when we turned into our own drive she seemed to hesitate. I tugged at her hand, for I wanted my tea. Then she smiled – but I remember thinking that it was a 'funny' smile – and ran with me to the house.

In the hall, as she was taking off her gloves, it happened.

What do I mean by 'it'? Something so small, so absurd, and tiny, that you may well laugh at me.

For 'it' was only a whistle.

Just my father, whistling softly, somewhere upstairs, a few bars of a popular song.

My mother became rigid. I can see her now, standing there, pulling the glove which seemed frozen to her hand. Behind her was a silver bowl filled with clusters of yellow berberis. The late sunlight flooded in through the door, lighting up her face which still had beauty, even though the beauty lay in shadow.

'I know what *that* means.'

She was speaking to herself. She had forgotten me.

She knew what the whistle meant, for he never whistled when he was sober.

And somehow, I knew what it meant, too.

'I know what *that* means.'

She said it again; she had forgotten me entirely; she was looking up the stairs, listening to the whistle. Slowly, flatly, with an imbecile intonation, it echoed towards us. It was coming nearer. Nearer, ever nearer. Then, at the top of the staircase, my father appeared. He was holding tightly to the banisters, and I noticed that he was rocking on his feet. As I saw his face I recognized another face – a face that in the

65

past year had come to me only in dreams, mixed up with dragons and devils – the face I had seen when he was lying on the floor, a year ago, with blood on his mouth and wine on his chest.

'I know what *that* means.'

It was not she who said it.

It was I who said it, in my heart.

II

The whistle, then, was Lesson Number One in the Child's Guide to Dipsomania. It meant 'He is beginning – look out!'

Sometimes, after a day of whistling, he would manage to pull himself together, and then there was a feeling of such peace and happiness as might come to a house that had been visited by an angel. But in nine cases out of ten, he went straight ahead. So we come to Lesson Two, which was concerned with the sense of smell.

The most odious aroma which I can imagine, in this world or the next, is the scent of a cream with which my father used to anoint the ends of his moustache. It was called *Pommade Hongroise*; it was made by Roget and Gallet, and a little mauve tube of it always lay on his dressing-table, between his ivory hair-brushes. It must be observed, in defence of Messrs Roget and Gallet, that there was nothing intrinsically obnoxious about the perfume, which was faintly tinged with vanilla and cloves. Its loathsomeness, to me, was entirely due to association. He used it lavishly at the beginning of a 'bout' and, with the strange detective instinct which I developed as a small boy, I could have told the stages of his drunkenness merely by studying the degrees of attenuation in the mauve tube on the dressing-table. When he was sober, the tube shrank slowly – when he was drunk it would be violently squeezed, and sometimes there would be flecks of cream on the mirror, where his trembling hands had spilled it. Often I have gone up and wiped it off with a towel before my mother could see it.

Other scents assail me, all concerned with the Second Lesson; not the scents of alcohol, but of the various unguents, toilet-waters and mouth-washes which he employed to cover up his tracks. These early antiseptic odours have a queer menace for me; particularly the scents of the bathroom, in which he used to spend hours crouched over the basin, fiddling with sponges for his bleary eyes and gargles for his parched throat; they drift down the years, as they once drifted down the corridors. In particular the scent of Glyco-Thymoline. Look at him, gargling like an animal at bay, the purple fluid matching the colour of his cheeks. The scent of eau-de-Cologne, wiped over his sweaty forehead, sprayed on the handkerchief which he stuffs, with a flourish, into his breastpocket.

Then he comes downstairs. Tea is waiting for him. The silver kettle, the piping scones, the little plate of sandwiches. My mother pours out tea. Somehow or other she finds something to say – something that is sensible, and happy, and impersonal – something that will break the tension and yet will not offend. He does not answer, but fixes her with a look of malevolence. He snatches his tea and drinks it greedily. There is the sound of liquid sucked through a moustache. And a sickly scent of *Pommade Hongroise,* strong Indian tea, and eau-de-Cologne.

III

So much for Lessons One and Two. Lesson Three . . . but this recital will become tedious. There were a hundred lessons, but they are for the 'expert'; the normal reader would scarcely understand them. I will therefore content myself with tabulating a few of those symptoms which may serve, firstly to show my own morbid sensitivity to his condition, and secondly to illustrate his character.

In his youth my father had been strikingly handsome. On the mantelpiece of my mother's bedroom stood a faded photograph in a silver frame. It showed him in rugger kit, sitting in an attitude of easy, almost arrogant grace, head thrown back, lips smiling, hands clasping a pair of muscular knees.

By no effort of imagination could I connect this gay and ardent image with the figure I knew in real life. From the age of forty-five onwards my father never weighed much less than fifteen stone; and he seemed to take pride in his *en-bonpoint*. When he was sober there were many bluff and hearty references to his stomach, many resounding pats upon it. Personally I found this distasteful; I shrank from this mound of flesh, not only because it was physically repulsive in itself, but because it was the outward sign of the indulgence which had caused so much misery.

However, we are concerned at this stage with clues; how did I come to learn, merely by looking at his face, if he were 'beginning'? The first clue, I think, would be his right eyebrow; it seemed to be twitched upwards, only a fraction of an inch, but quite enough to give a clear warning. Then after another double whisky, the left eyebrow would follow suit, giving him a curious expression of indignation.

One extraordinary detail should be recorded; he never mislaid his eyeglass until he was completely insensible. He wore it without a cord, and without a rim. It was a plain circle of glass which he adjusted instantly, without any effort, even when his hands were shaking violently. He was very proud of this accomplishment; sometimes, so he told us, young men in the street would nudge each other and point to his eyeglass, and one of them would make a rude reference to it; whereupon he would shout back 'Come and knock it out!'

If I have heard this story once I have heard it a hundred times. '"Come and knock it out," I said. That's what I shouted back . . . "Come and knock it out!"'

It is a sad little picture, the ageing, staggering figure, shaking his stick at the local youths, and going on his way, through the narrow streets of a provincial town, clamping his eyeglass more firmly into place.

Apart from the lifted eyebrows, the 'appearance clues' are almost too obvious to mention – they vary from his chin, scarred by the jerk of a trembling razor, to his trousers, stained by the overflow of liquor which he had drunk straight from the bottle. I can see him carving a chicken at table, and feel again the sense of dread with which I note the tell-tale grimace which puffs out his cheeks; or I can recall his habit of reading a newspaper with the pages so tightly gripped that they sometimes tear.

Yes, it was a sixth sense that I developed. Even when he was out of the room, I could tell his condition, by studying the creases of the chair in which he had been sitting. It sounds an impossible claim but it is unfortunately a true one.

Three more 'clues' will suffice; they each throw an interesting light on his character.

IV

Handwriting.

This was my chief source of information when I was away from home – at school or at the University. My mother's letters rarely hinted that anything was amiss; indeed, so cleverly did she conceal the facts, that for weeks, surrounded as I was by new interests and normal companions, I would be lulled into a sense of false security. But gradually I became more wary; I learned, for instance, that if he did not write at all, it was a sure sign that he was in the last stages, for he used every period of sobriety to indulge in correspondence with his diminishing circle of friends and relations, simply in order to show them that he *was* sober. He took great pains with these letters – making a rough copy of them and then tracing them in as firm a hand as possible.

After receiving one of these letters, in the firm handwriting, it was usually safe to assume that three or four days later I should receive another, in a handwriting not so firm, and so on, until a series of almost indecipherable scrawls announced the worst. I will not attempt an essay in dipsomaniac calligraphy, although it is hardly an exaggeration to say that even at the age of ten, I should have been able to tell, by the crossing of a single 't', the approximate amount of alcohol which the writer had consumed. However, I think it is legitimate to point out the inconveniences to which this disability subjected his household.

For example: there were many periods when he was incapable of signing a cheque. My mother never had a banking account; although the greater part of our family's money had come from her, it had all been transferred to my father. It was not till I was very much older that I realized this, and rebelled at the gross injustice of it – with results which were unexpectedly dramatic, as I shall have occasion to narrate. In the meantime, it is enough to observe that my mother never had a sixpenny piece (of her own money) which was not handed to her, in cash, by my father. And since he was so frequently incapable of any sort of action, she was often greatly embarrassed.

'Oh – if only he could sign a cheque!'

How often she said that, pacing the room, wondering what to do!

It was, when you come to think of it, a curious situation.

There, in the morning-room, sits my father at his desk, trembling from head to foot. He is in the 'remorse' stage, he is physically weak from days and nights of vomiting, and mentally abased by long and soul-racking scenes of remorse. He is back again in the world now, the cruel world of sunlight from which his whole life is an attempt to escape.

And he wants money. But he cannot get it.

The cheque book mocks him. A pink cheque book, on a Bristol bank. My mother has made it out – pay cash, twenty pounds. The cash is in the bank, all that is needed is his signature – John Nichols. Once again he dips his pen in the ink, places it on the paper, takes a deep breath, bites his lower lip. And once again, just as he thinks he is going to do it, his poisoned stomach contracts, and the pen is twitched from his hand. And he throws it down, and buries his head in his hands.

We may pity him. I did pity him. For many, many years, the long, long years of youth. Pity he had in plenty, and prayer, and patience. But there is an end to pity, and it is right that there should be an end; for there comes a time when it is a veil over the face of truth.

V

Gardening

Just as I could have told you my father's condition by studying the creases of a chair in which he had been sitting, so I could also have made a pretty accurate diagnosis by studying his tracks after he had been out in the garden. It was not a question of looking for footsteps on flower-beds, or anything as crude as that; it was a subtler matter.

For example, there would always be a pile of leaves and twigs, scattered on some remote path, to indicate that he had been clipping a bush. This was a very bad sign. The leaves were a mark of his indignation, they proclaimed 'See now I have been driven out of the house to work myself to death!' And the fact that they were in so obscure a position showed that he was not sure whether he was able to clip straight.

Normally, he did absolutely nothing in the garden; during the long summer evenings when my mother was bent double over the beds, weeding and watering and trimming edges with an old kitchen knife, he would be lolling in a chair, staring at the ceiling if he were drunk or reading a library book if he were sober. Ours was a very beautiful garden but it was far too large for our means; most of its upkeep devolved upon my mother.

My father seemed to take a perverse pleasure in the struggle she had to keep the garden from running to waste. '*You* wanted this damned house,' he would say to her. '*You* made me buy it.' (Incidentally, it was he who had chosen it, and it was her money which had paid for it.) 'You can take the consequences.'

Sometimes when he was feeling particularly amiable, he would mow the tennis lawn. This was a great event, and it had to be properly acknowledged; we were called out to observe how beautifully it had been mown, how straight the lines were, how gigantic the mound of grass which was heaped in the corner. All these tributes we dutifully paid; but they were not enough. At dinner that night there would always be a reaction, expressed in the phrase 'Your damned garden's killing me'.

Sometimes he not only said those words but wrote them, with suitable embellishments, on the backs of envelopes which he left about the house, propped against ornaments on a mantelpiece, or pinned to the carpet at the top of the stairs. Many years later I was to have a grim reminder of this custom. I was going through a trunk of old papers during the war, sorting out what might be sent to the salvage collectors. I came upon a bundle of foreign editions of my book *Down the Garden Path*. They looked very gay in their bright covers but it seemed mere vanity to keep them; I could not understand most of the languages in which they were written and so I put them aside. As I did so, out of the pages of one of them fluttered a faded piece of paper, inscribed with a pencilled message in very plain English:

YOUR BLOODY GARDEN IS KILLING ME.

As I read it I took a deep breath, as a man might do when he passes the gates of a gaol in which he has once been imprisoned; it was a breath of relief. I thought: 'You poisoned the gardens of my youth, you blighted the leaves and the flowers, but now I have escaped. I have made my own garden, into which you cannot follow me.'

And then I wondered . . . could he not follow me, even now? *Did* he not follow me, even now?

But these are morbid speculations; my only object, in this passage, was to point to that pile of leaves and twigs lying on the shaded path, and to remind you that it was by such symbols that my early footsteps were guided.

VI

Language

I have already indicated that my father had a brand of obscenity peculiar to himself; for obvious reasons it is impossible to give samples of its quality; and were it not for the fact that it was usually directed against my mother, I should not have cared much about it. There comes a time when foul words are simply so many sounds – animal sounds that mean no more than the barking of a dog.

However, there was one exception – a word which never lost its power to shock. Syphilis. Whenever my father was beginning a bout his conversation was liberally interlarded with reference to the disease of syphilis. When I remember that my mother was brought up in a strict Victorian household, and educated in a French convent where she was never even allowed to look upon a man, let alone speak to one – and when I remember that only a few years later she was listening to the hiss of this word from the twisted lips of the man whom she loved and to whom she had given children – but there are some things which it is better not to remember.

Yet I must recall this word, as calmly as possible, because it formed an essential note in the scale of my youth; it was struck again and again, in a thousand modulations. Syphilis was an obsession with my father, probably because his brother Arthur – as I have mentioned in an earlier chapter – had contracted it, and eventually died of it. Considering the crudity of the treatment available in those days he seems to have put up a pretty good fight, particularly as he was infected at a very early age.

My father, who had curious ideas of the subjects most suitable for the delectation of his sons, never tired of telling us the story of Arthur's trouble. He discovered it, apparently, during a football match. He and Arthur were having a shower after the game, and, in his own words . . .

''Pon my soul, there he was, with spots all over his chest the size of half a crown. "Can't think what's the matter," he said, "coming out in a rash like this," he said. "I can tell you what's the matter, old man," I said, "you've got syphilis. Secondary syphilis, that's what you've got." And sure enough, he had. Spots the size of half a crown they were, and a nasty dirty brown.'

Syphilis was, as I observed, something of an obsession with my father. Had he been a doctor he would probably have regarded it as the bginning and end of all the ills to which the flesh is heir; had he been a historian he would have seen in it the cause of the rise and fall of empires (as indeed it may well have been). Since he was only a provincial gentleman of leisure he contented himself with attributing it to all with whom he came in contact. Naturally all the members of his own family were accused, at one time or another, of having the disease; the circle broadened, my aunts had syphilis; it was written all over the letters of my remotest cousins; it was stamped on the handiwork of the gardener. Even a new housemaid would come under the ban.

Today, venereal diseases have lost much of their power to kill and most of their power to shock. Even so, syphilis was never a pretty thing, nor a pretty word, and from the lips of my father it sounded particularly foul, like the hiss of

74

a snake. 'Sshyphilis ... sshyphilis ... that's what's the matter with you, my boy ... sshyphilis.'

Such were the echoes that haunted the dreams of my childhood, and by now, surely, our Child's Guide to Dipsomania should be complete. Not quite. There is one other phenomenon to be noted – a very curious one; and though its significance may not be apparent till the end of our story we will describe it here, for it forms a pictorial background to all the scenes that follow. It may be given the heading of ...

Family Portraits

As a firmly middle-class family, whose origins could be established for only two generations, we could not boast of any ancestral portraits. There were only two pictures with any claim to authenticity – one of my mother, painted by an obscure Yorkshire academician when she was a girl, and another of a man who was described, I believe correctly, as 'Great-uncle Richard'. The first, though clumsily executed, caught some of the radiant sweetness of my mother's features, the second was not so pleasing. Great-uncle Richard had one of the most forbidding faces imaginable; he would have been well cast for the leading role in *The Barretts of Wimpole Street*, and if I had had any say in the matter he would have been banished to the attic.

However, at least these pictures were genuine in the sense that they were indeed connected with our own forebears. But they were not enough for my father, and slowly, as the years went by, they were joined by a collection of motley companions, who glowered down from the dark walls and over the heavy Victorian dressers, and eventually mounted the walls of the staircase, where their eyes followed one on the way to bed. He only bought these things when he was drunk. (The end of Stage One.) Next door to the Queen's Hotel there was an antique shop, and sometimes, when he was in what might be called an 'ancestral' mood, he would peer through the window, see a painting in the shadows, stumble through the door, and buy it. This gave him a keen sense of pleasure and achievement; it called for a celebration . . . he must have another double whisky and then a cab to take him home; luncheon must be put back and the picture must be hung without a moment's delay. Some of my mother's pretty water colours must be torn down to make a space on the wall, while she hurried to fetch the steps (his 'heart', of course, forbade himself to make this exertion) – and I was instructed to collect the nails and hold the string. After which he would stagger back, adjust his eyeglass, and give the picture a name.

Turning to me he would say . . . 'This is your Great-great-aunt Polly.' And then, when he noticed my mother smiling, he would snarl at her . . . 'Well, have you any comments?' And her smile would fade. There were so many of these portraits that I have forgotten all but two of the names he gave to them. One was an atrocious daub whose subject, he decided, was 'a French *marquise*'. (Presumably because she had white hair and a sort of crinoline.) The other was another Barrett of Wimpole Street character, with sepia whiskers and a slight squint. When he hung it up he leered at me from the top of the steps and said . . . 'A baronet, m'lad, but the wrong side of the blanket.' To my youthful understanding the phrase was meaningless, and I turned to my mother for an explanation. I didn't get it. For his voice was loud and raucous when he barked at her . . . 'This is Sir Lionel. And don't you forget it.'

Gradually these puppets became real to him – so real, indeed, that until I was old enough to see through the pretence they also became real to me. 'Polly' was indeed my great-great-aunt; the blood of the bastard baronet flowed in my veins; and in the tangled branches of an imaginary family tree I glimpsed the faded features of a French *marquise*. The influence of this rather macabre farce on my young mind is almost too obvious to be stated; it was yet another hindrance to my efforts to establish my own standards either

76

of art or of personality. I grew up in a dream world of my father's creation, and just as it was impossible to imagine a normal home, with open doors and sunlight flooding through the windows, so it was impossible to imagine a normal inheritance – where in later years one might stand by a grave, knowing that one had indeed a physical and spiritual link with those who rested in it. A grave, to me, became a repository of painted ghosts, and for many years those ghosts walked with me down the long corridors of life.

I suggested above that the black comedy of our ancestral portrait gallery had a special significance, which could not be revealed till nearer the end of this book. This is indeed true, for the story the pictures have to tell us is so strange that without a good deal of further explanation it would sound incredible.

Even so, I will give a clue to its nature as it was eventually revealed to me. I believe that the real John Nichols had already almost died, that he knew it, and that he was trying to fill the void with another sort of reality – that in his self-created loneliness he was seeking new vitality, like some creature of the dark, searching desperately for fresh blood to fill its emptied veins.

Chapter Six ~

It is time that the picture widened.

So far the light has been focused on only three figures, my father, my mother and myself – with a few others moving dimly against a dark background. Miss Herridge appeared for a moment, and I tried to paint her as the radiant figure she was; but somehow she seemed to be out of the picture. How could it be otherwise? She *was* out of the picture, and so was everybody else in the normal world. Our lives were painted on a poisoned canvas, pinched in a narrow, sombre frame, and everybody who was not in that frame seemed to be out of drawing.

It is for this reason, perhaps, that my brothers have not yet come to life; they were part of the prevailing darkness; they were so close that I did not see them. Later on I shall try to give them their due; Paul, with his deep spirituality and his thwarted brilliance, who was destined for the Church; and Alan, with his fierce strength and physical beauty, whose talents were to be blighted by sickness, but who never faltered in his kindliness nor his courage.

It was Paul, in the later years, who supported by far the greater part of the burden of my father; it was he who was destined to give an example of Christian forbearance and fortitude only too rarely encountered in ministers of the Gospel, not only during my mother's life-time but after her death. Since Paul, at the time these words are written, is very much alive, and since, as I know only too well, he will wish that the words had never been written at all, I will speak to him personally . . .

Dear Paul: You and I have been involved in this tragedy together, and we have reacted to it in totally different ways. You have accepted it, and again and again you have continued to forgive, while I have continued to condemn. Why?

After all, we are brothers, with much in common, spiritually and intellectually. Why is it that in myself the hatred still burns, while in you it seems to have died away, to have been resolved into some higher philosophy?

I will tell you one of the reasons. It is because – though you may not have realized this – I have always been angered by the thought of the extent to which your own life has been stunted by the man who brought you into the world. Whether you were truly destined for the Church is doubtful, but as a leader of men you might have been pre-eminent. Your talents were not directed to the arts, but as a preacher you were indeed an artist. I have heard most of the great preachers of our time, bishops, arch-bishops, evangelists; compared with yourself they were flat and halting. When you had a great congregation of men, as you sometimes had, there was an almost psychic rapport; the church seemed to light up with a strange radiance. But even when, only too often, your audience was sparse and scattered, you gave of your best and it was as inspiring as great music.

I will remind you of an episode that you may have forgotten, so poignant that I can scarcely bring myself to recall it. Your last incumbency was the little parish of Sennen, at the tip of Cornwall, which is within a few miles of the storm-lashed cliffs of 'Land's End' – a name that carried the echo of seagulls and the ceaseless swirl of Atlantic spray. As children, you will remember, we spent our holidays at Sennen, and it was in the gaunt granite rectory that we passed some of our few interludes of childish happiness. To this rectory I came one summer, many years later, to stay with you, to do some work, to keep you company, to gain comfort from your warmth and understanding. On the first Sunday of my visit I went to your church, where you were officiating. I sat in a cold, empty pew, and looked around me. The grey walls bore tablets and memorials to forgotten patrons, the wind swept against the cracked windows, the prayer-books were dusty and mildewed. There were seven others in the congregation, precisely seven, six women and one man, and they were not inspiring people; they were all elderly and they had come to church from habit rather than from conviction; they reminded me of the stunted bushes of thorn that clung to the distant cliffs. Then you stepped into the pulpit and spoke your sermon. It was pitched in a minor key but it was none the less compelling; you made no special effort because I was present; you spoke as you always spoke, and if the great ones of the Church could have heard you, they might perhaps have realized their own short-comings – they might perhaps have paid tribute to a master.

But as things happened, the great ones passed you by. The Reverend Paul Nichols departed from Sennen uncelebrated. The message he had to give, the music of the words in which he expressed it, has drifted over Land's End, and been lost at sea.

Or has it? Is any music ever lost? Are any of the melodies of man's spirit ever silenced? Is it all a mad, senseless mélange of discord, with the wind at the windows, and the cry of the sea-gulls outside?

To that question, on this side of the grave, there can be no answer. But when I remember you and your example, I feel that there must be an answer, and that it will be one of which we need not be afraid.

So the picture broadens, and the 'story' – if such a word can apply to these studies in madness – can continue. The clock moves forward three or four years; our house drifts back into perspective; and other houses come into view, standing proudly among the tall trees. We adjust our vision to this new angle and we see, moving about the gardens, in and out of the french windows the figures of various men and women, our neighbours.

As we study them, we are struck by surprise. We had expected everybody beyond the narrow frame of our own tragedy to be out of perspective, to be painted in different colours – colours which would distinguish them, by their brightness and normality, from the central composition of the Nichols' family group. But this has not happened. These people are not in the least out of the picture; they are lit by the same unreal and slightly sinister sheen in which we ourselves have been moving.

What does this mean? Are our neighbours tainted too? Are they *all* mad? Is this a haunted hill on which we are standing?

'Is this a haunted hill?'

It was my mother who said those words, one day, looking out of her bedroom window on a moonlit night of midsummer. We had just heard of the attempted suicide of one of our few friends, an old lady who lived a quarter of a mile away. She had sought her death in a manner so grotesque that it would have been comic if it had not been macabre.

This old lady, whom we will call Lady X, had suddenly decided that life was not worth living. She had therefore staggered out of bed, lifted herself on to the window-sill – she was gigantically fat – and attempted to plunge out of life. Unfortunately life, in this case, was rather too literally like Shelley's dome of coloured glass, so that she landed straight on to the roof of the Moorish conservatory, where she hung suspended over a girder, slowly bleeding to death. In the meantime her husband (another dipsomaniac), disturbed by the noise, had staggered out, and seen the strange apparition of his wife, sprawled across the heavens, moaning to herself. What did he do? He did three things. Firstly, he fetched a small cushion of pale blue satin, which he placed on the floor beneath the body. Secondly, he returned to the library and finished his decanter of port. Thirdly he telephoned to our house, and requested that my brother Alan (chosen because of his physical strength) should call immediately. He did not disturb the butler or any of the staff, because the butler was temperamental, and might not like such goings on.

This was the scene upon which Alan walked – Sir John, placidly reading in the library, waving his hand courteously towards the conservatory where his wife lay suspended, like a crashed balloon, her blood dripping slowly on to the pale satin cushion. Alan took the situation in his stride – after all, he was seventeen, the son of my father, and he was by now fully accustomed to such situations. But when he returned, having dragged the old woman back to safety, he looked very pale; there was blood on his hands, and his knees were badly cut with the glass.

'You ought to have a little brandy,' said my mother.

'No thank you, mother.'

'Just a very little.'

He shook his head. 'I'm all right.'

My mother kissed him goodnight; Alan was more than a boy, he was almost a young man; he was certainly entitled to a glass of brandy after such an experience. But I know that there was a deep thankfulness in her heart that he had not taken it.

It was on that night that she came to my room, when I was in bed, and looked out of the window, and whispered, more to herself than to me . . . 'Is this a haunted hill?'

II

I believe, quite honestly, that it was. Apart from the evidence of our family, I have solid grounds for this belief, of which you will learn in good time. There was madness in the air; the contours of the hill had the insane twist of a mountain seen through the crazed eyes of Van Gogh; there was a poison in the very soil of the luxuriant gardens around us, as if, long ago, they had been the scenes of hideous rites and cruelties, for which we had to pay a present sacrifice.

The picture broadens, yes. But it does not broaden into a normal design; it is lit with an ever wilder light, in which we make the acquaintance of an ever weirder horde of eccentrics.

Here they are – our neighbours of the haunted hill. I present to you:

Professor Oliver Heaviside. He was our immediate neighbour on the west. His name, of course, is pure Dickens; the man himself might have been created by Strindberg, elaborated by P. G. Wodehouse, and finished off by Edgar Allan Poe. At the time of my boyhood Professor Heaviside was engaged in certain intricate researches into the nature of etheric waves. I cannot describe his discoveries, but they must have been of some importance; when he died *The Times* published a long obituary about him, in which his name was coupled with Edison and Marconi.

But I could have told *The Times* a great many things about Professor Heaviside which, though they might not have been of interest to the scientists, would have provided the student of eccentric psychology with abundant food for thought. *The Times*, for instance, did not mention that he seldom dressed, and was usually attired in a kimono of pale pink silk. Nor did *The Times* see fit to mention that Heaviside, in a moment of pique, had caused most of the furniture of his house to be removed, and had replaced it by large granite rocks, which stood about in the bare rooms like the furnishings of some Neolithic giant. Through those fantastic rooms he wandered, growing dirtier and dirtier, and more and more unkempt – with one exception. His nails were always exquisitely manicured, and painted a glistening cherry pink.

Was Professor Heaviside mad? Presumably not – his scientific record shows him to have had a brain of exceptional range and delicacy; he was probably one of the few men of this century who could have argued intelligently with Einstein. But to me he was just another figure of whom to be afraid; he was surrounded with a childish aura of terror. Sometimes I used to creep under the bushes and peer through a gap in the wall, and watch him prowling about his ragged, thorny garden. Through the unwashed windows I could see the rocks, standing against the walls of his drawing-room. Now and then he would pause, and glare in my direction; he had a habit of suddenly pulling his pink dressing-gown very tight, and flicking his glistening fingers above his head.

We had no close contact with this singular character, but occasionally, during the summer months, my father would receive a letter from him on the subject of tennis balls which I, or my brothers, had inadvertently knocked into his gardens. These letters always began as follows:

His Wormship, Professor Oliver Heaviside, (W.O.R.M.), presents his compliments to Mr. John Nichols, and wormfully requests permission to bring certain matters to his attention.

Then came the substance of the complaint. The letters were always signed Oliver Heaviside, W.O.R.M. It is an ironic thought that the author of these letters was largely responsible for bringing radio technique to its present pitch of perfection.

My father thought Professor Heaviside was a grand joke, and doubtless he was. But to me, as a child, he was a bogy, a witch-doctor, another figure to fear in a world in which fear was the guiding force. Never would I venture into his garden, to fetch a ball that had been lost; I felt that once inside those walls I should never come out again . . . or if I did, that I should be changed, and have a light of madness in my eye, and should wander down the hill, and out into the world, a lost boy, whom nobody knew.

III

To the south dwelt old Miss Faithful.

The name, again, is Dickensian: the figure is Turgeniev with a touch of Mark Twain.

This may be crystallized in a single sentence; Miss Faithful was a rich and amorous dipsomaniac whose principal interest in life, apart from the bottle, was the care of sixteen laughing jackasses.

Now that I evoke these figures from my memory, and trace their outlines on paper, I find myself pausing, rubbing my eyes and asking: 'Did they really exist? Or am I confusing them with some distant nightmare?' I am afraid that there is no doubt of their existence; I can hear the sound of those laughing jackasses to this day. At the bottom of our garden, behind a deep shrubbery that bordered the tennis court, there was a high wall which separated Miss Faithful's estate from ours. It was somewhere behind that wall that the laughing jackasses were kept. They did not laugh very often; but sometimes towards dusk I would be playing by myself in the shadow of an immense cork tree, when the air would be rent by a shrill and lunatic cackle . . . ha ha ha, he he he, ho ho ho . . . on and on, like the screaming of a witch. I would pause, and grow pale, and stare around me . . . to the south, that hideous sound, to the west, the 'wormful' professor in his house of rocks . . . to the north, my drunken father . . . to the east . . . but we will not turn that way yet.

A normal boy would probably have climbed the wall and thrown a stone at those ominous birds. But what could I know of normality?

We will not pause long with Miss Faithful, we need only register her as just one more point in the compass of fear by which our house was surrounded. I suggested that she was a blend of Turgeniev and Mark Twain. Her death was an admirable example of this strange collaboration. At the end of a long bout of *delirium tremens* her servants left her *en masse*; only her faithful companion remained. She was obviously dying, but she would not see a doctor, so the companion sent in desperation for my father, as the nearest male. Since he was in the middle of a bout of *delirium tremens* himself, it was my elder brother Paul who went to the rescue. He was then about twenty-four and had just taken holy orders. He hurried down to the great rambling house, and was led through rooms in which half-starved cats and verminous dogs crept whining through the shadows. The stench, he said, was indescribable – the windows were filthy, the ceilings were festooned with spiders' webs. In the midst of this macabre setting lay Miss Faithful, her wig awry, her eyes glassy with drink and creeping death. But even at this late hour she was shaken by a last ghostly spasm of coquetry; she raised herself in bed and pointed to my brother. 'You are a brave young man,' she cackled, 'coming alone into a lady's bedroom. The world . . .' and here she was shaken by a gigantic hiccup . . . 'the world is so censorious.'

IV

Thus were we bounded on the west and the south. To the north, our nearest neighbour was more presentable, though even she could hardly be described as normal. Violet Tweedale was a statuesque woman of striking beauty. Her hair was the colour of snow lit by candlelight, and she had the majestic poise which we have come to associate with the late Queen Mary. She was rich, dominating, racy. And she produced an unending stream of atrocious novels, sometimes about earls and sometimes about ghosts, and usually about both.

I cannot say that I was frightened by Mrs Tweedale's earls, but her ghosts gave me the creeps. I had myself a lively imagination, more than adequate to people my youthful horizon with its quota of spectral phenomena, and when Mrs Tweedale, walking through the garden, would suddenly pause, point to the herbaceous border, and observe, in a deep booming voice . . . 'There are two elves climbing up that foxglove,' I found that my natural inclination to giggle was checked by a cold shiver. Maybe there *were* elves on the foxgloves, and what would happen if I were to tread on one without seeing it?

However, on the whole Mrs Tweedale was a comfort; her house was neither a lunatic asylum nor an inebriate's home, and that was saying a lot. The last time I saw her she was very old and inclined to wander, but she was still on intimate terms with elves; and the unseen world – (unless she was a fraud, which is possible) – was still more real to her than the seen.

She sat in a chair by the drawing-room fire and stared fixedly at a screen. 'What is that bright light moving about behind the screen?' she asked my mother.

My mother looked puzzled. 'I do not see one – there is only the maid.'

Mrs Tweedale nodded. 'Of course,' she said. 'Foolish of me. It is her aura. A very remarkable aura. Great spiritual force and a fiery imagination.'

I caught my mother's eye, and saw the laughter dancing in it. Since I am grateful to anybody who ever made my mother laugh, I think more kindly of old Mrs Tweedale than of most of the other ghosts that thronged our haunted hill.

And then there was 'Egie'.

V

I would like you to see Egie as I first remember him, before the shadows closed around him.

He was to suffer the tortures of the damned, to attempt suicide, to be shut in a mental home, and to escape from it – to sink into a gutter of sensuality and to die a strange and lonely death before he had reached middle age. His record, in other words, was typical of the haunted hill. But when I first saw him, he seemed enchanting.

He had come to call on my mother, offering his excuses for his parents, who were ill. (His real name, by the way, was Egerton Edwards.) He was about thirty, dark, pale, with a romantic cast of features that reminded me of a lithograph of Byron that used to hang in the billiards-room. He was remarkably elegant; he wore brown suède shoes with his white flannel trousers, and there was an orchid in the button-hole of his double-breasted jacket. A solitaire emerald glittered on the little finger of his left hand, and he smoked

Turkish cigarettes through a long black holder. He carried with him an immense bunch of dark red roses, which he handed to my mother with the sort of gesture that one sees in the elementary classes of schools for dramatic art.

I appear to have described a bounder; he was, as it happened, a gentleman, and in spite of his affectations, there was much in him that was lovable.

'I hope I shall see a lot of you,' said Egie to my mother.

But it was on me that his eyes were fixed. I am obliged to observe that I was not an ugly boy. However, the part that Egie was to play in my life, and in the general tragedy of the haunted hill, must be reserved for a later chapter.

Chapter Seven ❧

Egie was, of course, a homosexual.

It seems incredible, in these days, that my parents should not have guessed this. Towards the end, when his looks were fading, his face was heavily rouged, and the mascara on his eye-lashes was so thick that after a game of tennis, in which he performed with an erratic faun-like brilliance, his cheeks were streaked with dark rivulets. His clothes, his walk, the books he read, the company he kept – all these proclaimed, in language which would nowadays be comprehensible to any debutante, the abnormal man.

But though his homosexuality was blazoned all over him, my parents had no suspicion of it; if they had guessed, they would never have allowed him in the house. They – and I am afraid that in this case 'they' must include my mother – would have lashed themselves into that frenzy of artificial hysteria which still afflicted many otherwise tolerant people when confronted by examples of Nature's unorthodoxy. Their views on this subject were in every way 'correct' – in other words, in every way savage and primeval. Even my mother, in all other matters the gentlest and most understanding of women, would have applauded the outburst of the mother in the celebrated lesbian novel *The Well of Loneliness*. This person, on learning of the proclivities of her daughter, observed, in ringing tones, 'I would rather you were dead at my feet.' Once, many years later, I mentioned to my mother that I was going to a revival of *The Importance of Being Earnest* and asked if she would like to come too. She shook her head, and said she would not go to any play by Oscar Wilde.

'Mother, darling, isn't that a little extreme?'

'I would rather be in the same room with a snake than with Oscar Wilde,' she said. Which reminds me of a story that I shall be telling later.

My father, on the subject of Wilde, was even more fiercely bigoted, but he was equally obtuse in interpreting Egie's manifold eccentricities. Did he paint his face? How amusing! Was he seen in strange company, late at night, in the local inns? He was a 'Bohemian'! Did he openly proclaim his aversion to young women? He was a 'dark horse' and probably kept a mistress on the sly! And did he, from the outset, show an extraordinary interest in myself . . . asking me to dine, to go to concerts, giving me expensive presents? It was just his 'kindness'; he was eminently a 'nice' friend. His grandfather was a baronet, and his people moved in very respectable circles.

So it was, that when I was asked to dine at Warberry Court – (Egerton Edwards of Warberry Court – the names sound as though they had been invented by Ouida) – my parents were pleased to let me go. I was dressed up, for the first time, in my new dinner-jacket. An extra brush was given to my hair, which was very curly. Dinner was at eight, and I was told to arrive punctually at five minutes to; I was already dressed and waiting in the hall at half past seven.

'Please remember that his parents are both rather deaf,' said my mother. 'And don't ask anything about his relations because two of them are in lunatic asylums.' Which, of course, was only natural, on the haunted hill.

But his mother was not there, nor his father; there was nobody but Egie, waiting for me in a great drawing-room that was heavy with the scent of tiger-lilies. His people were in London.

It was a strange dinner to set before a schoolboy.

There was caviar and there was champagne. There was a mousse of chicken worthy of Brillat-Savarin. I forget the other dishes, but I remember that we ended with yellow chartreuse. I remember it because, by then, I was exquisitely drunk, and one's first intoxication is unforgettable. I leant back and apostrophized the gleaming fluid in my glass. It was gold, it was daffodils, it was the skin of tigers; it was the sands on which I had lain naked, it was sun-flowers, it was the hair of golden girls. I spoke my thoughts aloud.

'Girls?'

I looked up and I saw his face. He had risen, and was standing just behind me.

'Girls?' he repeated. His voice was thick and husky.

He began to run his fingers through my hair.

II

An hour later I was home again, lying hidden under the big cedar tree, looking up to the moon.

I wanted to think.

I was not horrified by Egie's onslaught; although his face, as he leant over me, had been lit by a passion which I suppose was 'unholy', it seemed less unholy than the frequent expressions of my father. And though, in adolescence, any sexual shock is disturbing to the nervous system, there are other forms of shock which are greater, and to these I had long been accustomed.

My main feeling – strange as it may seem – was one of disappointment. This was to have been my first dinner-party; for the first time in my life I was wearing a dinner-jacket, and, so I had fondly imagined, I would enjoy a normal evening, with normal people, and feel – even if only for an hour – like 'other people'. And this had been the result.

'*Are* there any "other people"?' I asked, lying there on the grass crumpling my new dinner-jacket even more than it had already been crumpled by Egie. '*Are* there any normal human beings, who drink water, and are not afraid of the police, and who, when they speak to one, speak neither with a curse nor a kiss?'

The moon had no answer. The moon, in any case, is an uncertain mentor for schoolboys, lying on the grass after such experiences, with their heads slightly muzzy from yellow Chartreuse.

That night I came to no decision. It was my father, not long afterwards, who brought things to a head.

III

In the meantime I continued to see a great deal of Egie, though I usually contrived that our meetings should be, as far as possible, by daylight.

With a precocious sagacity I avoided moonlight walks, the scent of tiger lilies, the music of Chopin, and all the emotional apparatus with which he desired to invest our friendship. To his declarations of passion I usually had some schoolboy riposte. He told me that I was breaking his heart, and sometimes he unbosomed himself in love-letters of singular sickliness – letters which contained copious quotations from almost every homosexual author who has ever set pen to paper, from Shakespeare to Walt Whitman.

For the rest, he was a charming and sympathetic companion; he shared my love of Mozart, and his artistic taste was austere, if not astringent, which was an excellent corrective for my own early enthusiasms. It was only in literature that he was unselective, because he was attracted by any characters which reflected his own abnormality. The golden trumpets of Shakespeare's sonnets – the scrannel pipings of Wilde's songs – they moved him to equal rhapsodies.

The mention of Wilde brings me back to my father and the continuation of our story.

One day, several weeks after the dinner which I have been describing, a small parcel was delivered at the front door. It was done up in fine white paper and silver ribbons, and to one of the ribbons was pinned a white rose. I recognised Egie's handwriting, and ran upstairs to undo the parcel in my own bedroom. It was lucky that I did so, for had my father known the contents and observed the manner of their delivery, even he might have begun to wonder if Egie was, after all, a very desirable companion for his son.

The parcel contained *The Picture of Dorian Gray*. It was an exquisite edition, in white parchment, embossed with silver fleurs-de-lis. I was so excited that I was on the point of running off to show it to my parents; then some instinct made me pause. I knew nothing at all about Wilde; I had not even heard the usual schoolboy limericks about him; in spite of my precocious knowledge of so much of life's seamy side I was absurdly innocent. But I had developed an animal capacity for scenting danger in the air and here, I felt, lay danger.

So I did not take the book to show to my parents. Instead, I locked the door, flung myself on the bed, and began to read.

It seemed to me the most wonderful book I had ever known. I was fifteen, remember, and at that age one is not an expert in imitation jewellery. Besides, are all the jewels of Dorian Gray so false? They may be only semi-precious, but to this day they hold in their depths a curious glitter, and they were mounted by a master-craftsman.

I read on and on, drifting from Lord Henry Wooton's lilac-scented studio to scenes of luxury that were all the more dazzling because they were set so close to scenes of squalor, devouring epigrams as greedily as I would have devoured a bowl of sweets, and thrilling to the soft and insistent rhythm of the theme of Sin – for that was what it was, though the true quality of the sin evaded me. The book moved me as though it were a melody to which all the themes of life were subtly modulated. I often think that Wilde was himself shocked by Dorian Gray when he was writing it, which is why it still retains its power to shock others. He was as conscious of sin as he would have been of some forbidden perfume; he did not breathe it carelessly; it was not part of the common air of his life; and though he sought it, and savoured it to the full, it was always a luxury to him, for which he knew he would have to pay, to the last drop.

I read on; the sunlight climbed up the walls and grew dim; the shadows lengthened in the garden, a cool breeze fluttered the curtains and caused me to get up, still reading, and throw a dressing-gown over my flannels. (I remember wishing that it had been like one of Dorian Gray's dressing-gowns, of peacock-green and silver.)

Suddenly, there was a knock on the door.

I started and closed the book.

'Open the door! What the devil's going on in there?'

It was my father's voice; and it brought me back, with a shock, from the world of pleasure to the world of pain.

He rolled into the room, glaring round him as if he had expected to find me closeted with some undesirable female. Then he sat down heavily on the bed. He was in Stage Two, the half-bottle-of-whisky-a-day stage, which did not make him drunk, but inflamed his liver and poisoned his brain.

'Locking the door, eh?'

'I'm sorry. I didn't know it was locked.'

'Didn't know it was locked? Ha! Ha! That's bloody funny.' He folded his arms, lifted his head, and stared at me with a glassy grin. Then the grin faded, and his face grew dark. He took out his monocle and polished it. Then he stuck it in again, and stared once more.

'Well?' he demanded.

I stood there, trembling. It was not a physical fear; I should not have minded if he had been going to beat me. I had been thrashed at school, in pyjamas, and though it was unpleasant it was bearable if you gritted your teeth. But this was different. It was, I suppose, the old familiar fear of madness; I knew that in the eye that glittered behind the monocle there was no sense, only a bitter, wide-ranging malevolence, and that in his brain a devil was enthroned, prodding him on to do evil in any way he could.

'Locking out your father, I suppose? Too grand for your poor old father, what?'

'I really didn't know . . .'

'Don't tell lies,' he snarled. 'I don't like liars. And I don't like sneaky things done behind locked doors.'

He stared at the carpet, shaking his head. There was a long pause – how often have I stood there like that before him, waiting, wondering, dreading!

His mood changed. He leant forward and chuckled.

'You're getting quite a big boy now, aren't you?'

His eyes swept over me; they seemed to undress me.

'Nice curly hair, like your mother used to have. Good pair of shoulders on you. A fine figure of a boy.' He nodded to himself. 'Yes.'

I turned away and pretended to tidy up the dressing-table.

'But it isn't right for growing boys to lock themselves up in their bedrooms all day. They may get into bad habits.'

I did not reply.

'D'you hear me?' He was shouting again. 'D'you understand?'

'Yes, I understand.'

'Good.' He relapsed into silence. I could hear his heavy breathing.

'Not right,' he muttered again. 'Not right.'

I heard the bed creak as he lurched off it. I heard two heavy steps. And then . . .

'What's this?'

I turned round. He was holding my book in his hand.

'It's . . . it's a book.'

'Where d'you get it?'

'I . . . I bought it.' Thank God that Egie had not written his name in it.

My father took out his monocle and polished it. Then, swaying from side to side, he held the book up to the light

95

and read out the title, very slowly and thickly. '*The – Picture of – Dorian – Gray*. By – Oscar . . .'

Then he seemed to choke. The purple deepened on his fat cheeks. He turned to me with an expression of such murderous hate that I stepped towards the wall.

'You filthy little bastard!' he screamed.

'Father . . .'

'Don't you dare speak to me . . . you . . . you scum!' He hurled the book at my head. It crashed against the mantelpiece, bringing down two little ornaments of which I was very proud. The noise of their breaking seemed to sober him for a moment.

'Pick that book up!'

I picked it up.

'Give it to me!'

I handed it to him. As I did so he struck me across the mouth.

'Now . . . you pretty little bastard . . . you *pretty* little boy . . .' (and as he said the word 'pretty' he sent his voice high and shrill, in a parody of the typical homosexual intonation) . . . 'watch me!'

I watched. My father opened the book, very slowly, cleared his throat, and spat on the title page. Having spat once, he spat again; the action appeared to stimulate him. Soon his chin was covered with saliva. Then, with a swift animal gesture, he lifted the book to his mouth, closed his teeth over some of the pages, and began tearing them to shreds.

Suddenly he threw the book from him, and ground his heel into it. For a moment he said nothing; he just stood there swaying, and breathing as quickly as if he had run a race.

Then he said . . . 'Oscar Wilde! To think that my son . . . Oscar Wilde!'

'But, Father . . . I don't understand . . .'

'You don't understand?' He stared at me owlishly. I

was quick to recognize the change in the tone of voice – the snarl had gone out of it; it was soft and maudlin. Now was my chance . . .

'No, Father. Honestly I don't.' And indeed, I could conceive no crime that could possibly cause any man's name to be so hated. 'What did Wilde do?'

'What did he *do*?' He shook his head; the crime was too terrible to pass his lips. 'Oh, my son . . . my son!' he groaned. And sinking on to the bed, he burst into tears.

That night, at dinner, my father was quite amiable. He kept on leaning over the table and winking at me, as though we shared some secret joke. I wondered how long the mood would last.

I was soon to know.

'Are you awake?'

I rubbed my eyes, and stretched. It was very early on the following morning; through the open curtains I could see the grey sky of dawn.

'Are you awake?'

I stretched again. I had been dreaming of Dorian Gray, and as Wilde might have said in one of his more extravagant moments – my dream had been as the shadow of a white rose in a silver mirror. Why must it be broken?

My father shook me by the shoulder, and I sat up. What on earth could he want with me at this time of the morning? Presumably it was going to be something unpleasant, for he was very flushed, and his eyes were puffy. There was an ugly growth of stubble on his chin, and he wore an old brown dressing-gown which revealed, all too clearly, his bulging stomach.

'Good morning, Father.'

He grunted and scowled at me.

'Got a pencil?'

'Yes. What for?'

'Never mind what for. Where is it?'

'In the top right-hand drawer of my desk.'

He lurched across the room, found the pencil, sat down, and began to write. It was all very mysterious, but I knew better than to make any comment.

He was writing very slowly.

'Printing capitals,' I thought to myself. He always printed capitals when his hand was shaky.

Curiosity was too strong for me. 'What are you writing?' I asked, taking care to make my voice sound apologetic.

'You'll see,' he said.

Then he drew a line, and threw down the pencil.

He got up and faced me, folding his arms.

'I've written what that man did.'

'What man?'

His face darkened.

'Don't pretend you don't know who I mean.'

'But I don't.'

'Wilde!' he barked. 'Oscar Wilde!'

'Oh!' I said. And then, to gain time, for I was still mystified . . . 'What he did?'

'It's unfit for a decent man to say.'

I took a fleeting glance at him. I thought – If it's unfit for *you* to say, what can it possibly be?

He went on: 'So, I've written it in Latin.'

He pointed to the desk and stumped to the door. 'And kindly remember this, young man. If ever I catch you reading a book by that man again, or if ever I so much as hear you mention his name, d'you know what I'll do?'

I shook my head.

'I'll cut your liver out! That's what I'll do. I'll cut your liver out!'

With which he removed himself.

For a moment I stayed in bed. I felt that some extraordinary revelation awaited me, over there on the desk, some strange secret knowledge of a nature so disturbing that after I had mastered it I should never be quite the same.

Then I threw back the sheets, tiptoed across the room, and picked up the piece of paper.

This was what he had written: ILLUM CRIMEN HORRIBILE QUOD NON NOMINANDUM EST.

I whispered the words to myself. ILLUM CRIMEN HORRIBILE – 'that horrible crime' – QUOD NON NOMINANDUM EST – 'which is not fit to be named'.

But what *was* it? What was I supposed to infer from that? I felt empty and cheated. Instead of raising the curtain, my father had only given it an extra tug. And behind it he had conjured up all sorts of hideous ghosts that were to torment me for a long time to come.

This was, to say the least of it, a singular initiation into the mysteries of sex, though it was very much in keeping with our life on the haunted hill.

But it had one good effect; it compelled me, at a very early age, to form an adult judgement on the whole vexed question of sexual abnormality. I had only two standards to guide me. The first was personified in Egie; and he was associated in my mind with music and laughter, with Shelley and Mozart, and, of course, with the purple prose of Wilde. The other standard was my father; and he meant blood and tears, and still more blood. Society kicked Egie into the gutter, because he was 'abnormal'; society accepted my father, because he was 'normal'.

Very well. If that was how society felt about these matters, I should take the liberty to differ.

Chapter Eight ✽

It was not long after the episode of *The Picture of Dorian Gray* that I attempted to murder my father. The attempt was, unfortunately, unsuccessful.

Of all the failures in my life, and there have been many, this is the one that I regret most keenly. Had I succeeded I should have had no spark of pity or remorse; my sleep, for many years would have been easier. As Wilde said, through the lips of Lord Henry . . . 'All the great crimes of the world are committed in the brain.' (Perhaps he had forgotten that Christ on a previous occasion had expressed the same conviction.)

In my brain I murdered my father, not once, but many times.

However, it was not through the influence of literature or religion that my thoughts were turned in this direction; it was through the impact of life. Usually the cause was some particularly cruel insult to my mother. To see *her*, with her gentleness, her selflessness, being worn down by ceaseless cruelty; worst of all, to be told by her that on no account must even a shadow of disapproval be shown towards him because of the old argument – 'it's a disease' – here was an ordeal of mental torture which was too much for any youth of sensitivity.

This chapter may have some interest to students of juvenile delinquency. Even in these comparatively enlightened days one reads in the newspapers of cases, usually in the homes of the working classes, where some boy, provoked beyond endurance by the bestiality of a drunken father, has taken the law into his hands, and in a fit of piteous, childish passion, has taken the life of his tormentor. We no longer put children behind bars; instead, we 'correct' them in barren institutions, we 'treat' them with psychiatric procedures, we do everything but understand them. But then, maybe such understanding is, and always will be, beyond the capacity of those who have not personally experienced, as children, the terrors and tortures which I am recording.

II

The attempt at murder had a specific cause which, for once, was not connected with my mother. But long before that, I had seriously considered how it might be possible to do away with him. I will try to recapture the brooding atmosphere of those early essays. They are always linked in my mind with long hot summer afternoons. Perhaps this is because it was only at such times that the house was quiet and deserted, with my mother resting in the garden, and the servants – when there were any – dozing in the kitchen, far away. My father, drunk or sober, was always asleep between two and four. This habit doubtless contributed to his deplorable longevity.

Whatever the reason for this association of murder and midsummer, my memory of the facts is clear. I would creep softly upstairs, and open the door of the great bedroom. The green velvet curtains, drawn against the sun, would billow out into the room, and then relapse with a sigh, as though they were saying, '*You* here again, you foolish boy? What do you expect to find, that was not here before?'

I could not have answered that question. But in that room, in cupboards, on the dressing-table, and on the old marble wash-stand, there were many medicine bottles, some of them marked 'Poison'. And it comforted me to let my fingers stray over those bottles, to take them up and stare at the labels and to think that here might be a way of release.

But usually, before I indulged in the luxury of examining the bottles, wondering how, and when, and where I might play the role of a Borgia, I would pause and fix my eyes on the open window. Through that window lay another way to murder. The ledge was low with a drop of twenty feet to the stone terrace beneath. I can see it still, and framed in it I can see the ectoplasmic outline of my father, whom I would push . . . push . . . push to death. I would stare at that frame, outlined by the sighing curtains, with all the glory of summer beyond it and slowly the figure would come into focus. The figure was always clad in a night-shirt, the most repulsive of draperies, which my father invariably affected. The figure was even grosser, in its spectral edition, than in real life, as though it had gained substance from my hatred. Maybe the very grossness of this ghost defeated me. I saw . . . yes, I *saw* . . . the folds of fat, the hairy legs, the bead-button eyes, I felt the clammy flesh of his buttocks as I struggled to push him over. The physical repulsion was too great. The figure faded, the window cleared and through it came the scent of roses.

The window is still there, in my brain. The figure is still there, too, in all its grossness, framed for eternity.

III

I began to be more specific.

On one of his frequent visits, the family doctor reproved my father for taking four tablets of aspirin. 'In your present condition,' he said, 'it is putting a strain on your heart.' Here, I thought, was a method in which I might well make some experiments – the classical tradition of the over-dose.

Fate was kind, on that long summer holiday which marked the beginning and the climax of my efforts. My brothers were both away; our staff had been reduced, by one of the recurrent financial crises, to a single maid, of a somnolent disposition. It therefore devolved upon me to take up the tray containing my father's evening meal, which was usually some form of soup or broth, as he could not eat anything solid.

Here, then, was a chance. I bicycled over to the neighbouring town of Newton Abbot, and purchased a bottle of aspirin from an obscure chemist. I chose a market day, for safety's sake, and as I entered the shop I held a handkerchief over my face as though my nose were bleeding, and turned away my head as I handed the money across the counter.

From this bottle, which I hid in an old pair of shoes, I extracted sixteen tablets of five grains each, making a total dose of eighty grains. This was four times the amount against which the doctor had warned him.

Just before the bell rang for dinner, at seven-thirty, I took a tooth-glass, crushed the tablets to a powder, and poured water on them. Then I ran downstairs and concealed the glass behind a bowl of flowers. It would be an easy matter to take it up with the tray, to pause outside the door and to mix the aspirin with the broth.

Everything seemed to be working perfectly; I felt calm, almost disinterested, and certainly in no way guilty. Does any man feel guilty when he strikes at the fangs of a snake, particularly when the snake is creeping towards one he loves? As I took the tray from my mother I smiled. 'You are very cheerful this evening,' she said. I nodded and went out whistling. I remember that I whistled the first few bars of an intermezzo by Brahms; I also remember that the glass containing the aspirin had been hidden behind a silver bowl filled with fuschias, and that a single scarlet petal had fallen into it. It was the work of a moment to mix the drug. A few seconds later I had opened the door and was standing by his bed.

Good. He was sitting up, which meant that his great body would not have to be heaved into position. He looked even more repulsive than usual, for he was feeling sentimental. At any moment he might break into the familiar, maudlin theme of 'I'm no good to anybody . . . I'm a bad father . . . you'd be better off without me . . .' – a theme which always reduced my mother to tears. Studying his face, which I hoped would soon be twitching in its last convulsions, I thought of the picture of Dorian Gray, and the subtle line of hypocrisy which had been the first sign of corruption to fall across the canvas.

'You're too good to me,' he moaned, holding out his hands.

Better than you guess, I thought.

Usually, when he absorbed his soup, I turned away, even at the risk of spilling it. I have always been physically fastidious; too easily nauseated by the leprous side of Nature's face; at the sick-bed and in hospitals I am a coward. But on this occasion I watched every detail with pleasurable attention – the red, loose lips closing over the edge of the bowl like some questing slug, the gulp, gulp of the thick neck – even the drops of fluid that congregated on the fringe of his moustache.

He lay back, licking his lips, sucking in the last drops.

'Too good to me,' he murmured.

Should I stay and watch? No. There might be unpleasant manifestations. I carried the bowl to the wash-stand, swilled it with water, and tiptoed out of the room.

'He drank it all,' I said to my mother, when I returned to the dining-room.

'Let's hope so.'

'Shall we have some music? Would it disturb him?'

'Not if you play softly.'

I played the first movement of Beethoven's Moonlight Sonata, for this is a piece which any intelligent child can play with his eyes shut, and my fingers had begun to tremble. After that I played some of the transcriptions of César Franck's organ chorales; they had a piercing purity; they built ladders of song to the throne of God. One had the right to such music, at such a time.

Then the dream was broken; there was a cry in the distance.

My mother started to her feet.

I stopped playing. 'What is it?'

'I thought I heard something.' She was looking up towards the ceiling.

'It was nothing.'

'Yes . . . there it is again. I must go to him.'

I put my hand on her arm: I was playing for time; every second counted now; the longer he was left alone the greater chance that he would die.

'You'll only distress yourself,' I said.

'I can't help that.'

'Let *me* go, for once.'

'You . . . you really want to?'

'I'll see to everything.'

I sped up the long dark staircase; panic was close on my heels, but even so, there was hope as well. 'Oh, God, please let him die!' I whispered. 'Please let him die!'

I flung open the door.

He was sitting on a chair in the middle of the room, clad only in a shrunken vest. He was tugging on his boots.

I stood in the doorway, open-mouthed. What had happened? My eyes wandered from him to the bed, where I had expected to see his corpse.

Then I understood. The bed was not a pretty sight; he had been violently sick. Whatever had been inside him a few minutes ago was certainly there no longer.

I wanted to laugh and to cry; most of all, with that beastliness a few feet away, I wanted to be sick myself.

'Clear up that bloody mess.'

I gulped. 'Yes, Father.'

He looked up with a start; I had been standing in a dim light and his back had been half turned to me; he had been under the impression that he was addressing my mother.

'Oh, it's you, my dear?' he whined, with a quick change

of tone, for he was cadging for favour. 'I'm afraid I've been rather ill.'

'So I see.'

'Can't think what it was. Perhaps it was the soup.'

'D'you feel better now?'

'Quite all right . . . quite all right. Thought I'd come downstairs for a bit.'

I went to clear up the mess.

On the following day my father was in very good spirits. He walked for two miles in the early morning, devoured an enormous breakfast, and in the afternoon he rolled the lawn.

So ended my first attempt at murder. There were to be others, but never again would I try my luck with any sort of poison. It was like trying to poison an ox. This man's stomach – apart from being stronger than steel, must obviously have a special technique of its own, merely through his extraordinary capacity for vomiting. He had trained himself to be sick as easily and as casually as the average man would comb his hair.

IV

My second attempt to murder my father came only a few weeks afterwards; and it was very nearly successful.

It was due to a dog.

My father hated dogs; he seemed to regard them as his special enemies; even in the street he would scowl and mutter at them, and often – if they were unaccompanied, throw stones at them.

Sometimes, from a distant garden he would hear a faint sound of barking, and then, beside himself with rage, he would rise from his chair and stalk out on to the terrace. For a moment he would pause, listening, staring about him, sniffing the air. Then his voice would break out in a hoarse shout . . . 'Stop that filthy noise! Stop it, you cur! Shut your filthy mouth!' His voice seemed to echo right down the valley. This habit did not tend to sweeten our social relationships.

There was never any argument about having a dog; we never said: 'Father, couldn't we have a puppy?' That would have been quite unthinkable. Even a hint of such a desire would have caused a volcanic eruption, and have been given as an excuse for weeks of surliness and excess.

The average man may find it difficult to realize the extent to which these early inhibitions may persist in later life. Here is an example.

Years later, at the age of thirty, I was sitting with a friend in the garden of my country cottage. The evening was golden, the meadows were bathed in sunlight, the air was sweet with lilacs. I lay back and counted my blessings. Many friends, an adorable garden, two charming houses, freedom to travel where I pleased – above all, work which was not only pleasant but profitable. What more, failing a wife, could a man desire? My friend supplied the answer.

'Of course there's only one thing lacking here.'

'What's that?'

'A dog.'

Before I realized what I was saying I replied: 'But I couldn't possibly have a dog.'

'What do you mean – you couldn't have a dog?'

What *did* I mean? How could I explain that dogs belonged to a totally different world, a world of wide spaces and open skies and fresh winds – a world that even now I could only see, as it were, through a window – framed in some form of art, but never with my open eyes, as part of one's natural heritage.

He spoke again. 'D'you mean a dog would spoil the garden?'

'No. I didn't mean that.'

We did not pursue the subject. But a great idea had been born, the idea that I might actually buy, own, and love a dog, and if I was very good, and worked very hard, and tried my utmost, might one day be loved by a dog. It was an idea of quite revolutionary import. I was a tax-payer, and a super-tax-payer, an employer of labour and an owner of property. But the thought of going and buying a bundle of wool, brown, black or grey – a bundle that would bounce about and bark and follow me – this was a joy that could not be imagined.

It was a joy that I was soon to know; I will not describe it, as I have already paid tribute, in another book,* to the only dog I have ever owned. For five years this dog was part of my life, and a very happy part; but even when my father was a hundred miles away, even when the dog and I had wandered together into a distant valley, and were running and laughing along the edge of a favourite wood, where the bracken grew golden and the foxgloves clustered thick – even then I had a feeling of guilt, as though we were being followed. 'You have no right to this new friend,' somebody seemed to whisper, 'he has no part in your life.' And then I felt that his cheerful bark was waking ancient echoes, in which a hoarse voice shouted 'Stop that filthy noise!'

Perhaps this was the reason that when my dog died I never got another.

However, all this sounds dangerously like self-pity, than which no mood is more tedious and more barren; besides, it is keeping us from our story.

My second attempt to murder my father, I said, was due to a black mongrel puppy. This was how it came about.

A few weeks after the episode of the aspirin, something happened that, in our family, was quite unique. My mother went away for a short holiday.

To this day, I cannot imagine what impelled her to this startling departure from practice, which had never occurred before and was almost never, during the rest of her life, to

* *A Thatched Roof.*

occur again. She had an acute nervous dread of leaving him alone; whatever trials she might have to endure by his side were as nothing to the imaginary horrors which she conjured up when she was absent.

For once in a way she decided to risk it. She was partly persuaded to do so because of the urgent necessity for resuming contact with our pitifully small circle of friends and some of our relations; during the past few years, for obvious reasons, they had not been invited to our home. And then, there was another reason. Ironically enough, ever since my attempt to murder him, my father had remained not only sober but almost amiable. He was positively recognizable as a member of the human species. It was as though all that had been needed to put him on his feet was a fatal overdose.

So she decided to go.

'You will be nice to him?' she pleaded. 'For all we know he *may* be quite all right.'

'I'm sure he will.'

'But if he isn't, you'll send me a telegram?'

'Only if he's really bad.'

She sighed. 'You'll have to be the judge of that. Don't send for Doctor Walker unless it's something desperate. And if he begins again, don't let him go out, whatever happens. Put it by his bed. You know where I've hidden it?'

'Yes. Inside the grandfather clock.'

The arrival of the hired carriage prevented any further instructions.

When the cab had vanished through the gates, I turned back into the house. Now that my mother had gone, my main feeling, strangely enough, was one of intense relief. Only now did I realize how greatly the effect of my father's cruelty was intensified by the fact that it was always directed at *her*: If I or my brothers had been the sole target of his attentions, we should have laughed in his face. What would it have mattered? We could have turned a blind eye to the more revolting physical manifestations . . . as for the slow dribble of blasphemous abuse, we should have regarded it as a compliment. You cannot be hurt by the disapproval of one whom you utterly despise.

So it was with a light heart that I turned towards the garden, where my father was sitting reading a newspaper. Almost I hoped for a trial of strength; almost I would have been glad to hear the sinister whistle that would have warned me that he was 'beginning again'.

Instead, I heard something else. A thin, sad little whimper, just behind me.

I looked round and saw a small black puppy, of dubious origins, half spaniel and half . . . what? It must have wandered through the front door, and it was creeping forward on its belly. It was wagging its tail feverishly, and gazing up at me with big brown eyes which seemed, in the heart-rending language of the mongrel, to be apologizing for its existence.

I stepped towards it. As I did so it shrank away from me as though it were afraid of being beaten. Very gently I picked it up, and held its paw which was bleeding. Always it stared at me with those piteous eyes.

I held it to me, trying to think of some plan of action. Here, within a minute of my mother's departure, was a situation of revolutionary import. Some instinct told me that I was going to keep this puppy, that nothing would ever part me from it but death. At the same time, it was worse than useless to ask my father's permission – in imagination I could see his cheeks flushing with rage at the very suggestion.

Even as I stood there, I heard his step on the terrace. There was not a second to lose. I covered the puppy with my jacket, hurried through the front door, and hid in the shrubbery. I heard my father's voice calling to me; then there was silence.

The puppy began to whimper again. 'Ssh!' I whispered. It was a very tiny whimper but my father had keen hearing.

The whimpering stopped and the puppy began to lick my hand. More than ever I swore that I should keep him.

But where? Then I remembered the old coach-house. Of course, that was the very place. The coach-house formed one side of a courtyard that straggled away from the servants' quarters. It was a fair-sized building which, in the old days, long before our time, had provided accommodation for four horses and two carriages, with rooms above for the coachman's family. Today it was empty except for a few pieces of lumber, and nobody ever went inside it. It was far enough from the house to be reasonably safe.

Thither I bore the puppy, and placed him in an old box of sacking that lay in a dark corner. He promptly curled up and went to sleep. I bent over him, marvelling at the adventure that had suddenly befallen me. 'I shall call you Peter,' I whispered to him. 'Peter.' He opened one eye for a moment, as though acknowledging his baptism, and then once again he fell asleep.

I tiptoed out and shut the door. And now – what was the next step? Obviously, I could not hope to keep him concealed without some outside assistance. The only person who could help me was Mary, the cook, who was our only remaining servant, apart from the odd man.

So into the kitchen I went, to plead with Mary.

Mary was rolling pastry. When I blurted out what had happened, she dropped the rolling-pin, her mouth opened wide, and she gasped, 'Lord help us, Master Beverley! What will *he* say?'

'He must never know, Mary.'

'But how can we keep it from him?'

In whispers we began to discuss ways and means. After a while we went out together to the coach-house to look at Peter. As soon as Mary saw him I knew that I had won. She had a warm heart; she swore that whatever happened, Peter would stay.

'And I'll tell you what,' she said. 'If *he* ever finds out, I'll say he's mine. Oh, of course, he won't be mine, Master Beverley,' she added hastily, seeing my crestfallen expression. 'He'll be yours, all yours. But I'll *say* he's mine, just to save trouble. What's more, I'll say that if he goes, I go. And maybe that'll make your father see reason.'

I shook Mary's floury hand. For the moment, all seemed well.

Two days later my father 'began again'. He began rather more quickly than usual and the first stage which usually lasted for five days, was over in twenty-four hours. This was largely due to my intervention. I wanted him out of the way, and as soon as I saw him beginning, I went to the grandfather clock, took out the whisky, and put it by his bed. Why not? Once he had begun, nothing would stop him. What was the use of pleading and cosseting? Why not get the wretched thing over . . . till the next time?

So there he was, safe in bed; and, apart from an occasional groan, everything was in order.

Now began a brief season of bliss, that lingers in my memory like a distant twilight – the bliss of a boy with his dog, running through the country lanes on a summer evening. Peter's paw healed quickly, and soon his puppy's brain healed as well; no longer did he crawl and flinch as though he were always in fear of a blow; instead he laughed – as puppies should – and bit my hand, and seized twigs and growled over them.

The days sped by; I wrote to my mother that all was well, explaining that my father could not write himself because he had sprained his thumb. I feared that she might realize that this was only an excuse, but somehow, nothing seemed to matter now that Peter was here. I had a shopping-basket that was strapped to the handlebars of my bicycle, and into this I used to lift Peter, like a baby, and strap the cover over him so that his head peered out and his long ears flapped in the wind.

I shall never forget our last evening together. I decided

to show Peter the sea. It was a scorching day; when we set out at six the sun was still high enough for several hours of delight. Soon we were at the top of the high cliffs that swoop to Babbacombe Bay. Oh . . . the joy of that long, breathless scramble . . . down, down, down . . . with the wild rock roses blooming in the hollows, and the tang of the wild thyme, and the tinsel clusters of the little flower called 'thrift'! As I tripped and tumbled through the undergrowth, clutching at any stunted branch that gave support, Peter's joyous yelps rent the air. Now and then I paused, breathless, and he leapt into my lap, a bundle of ecstasy. The world was winged . . . I had only to open my arms and together we would fly like birds to the blue and silver floor of the sea.

It was too good to last. Even as we were climbing down the cliff, a darkness was rising from the west; when we reached the beach the waves were already frisking in a sudden wind, and soon the first big drops on the scorched pebbles announced the breaking of the storm. We took shelter in a cave, Peter crouching at my side, trembling, and looking up at me after every clap of thunder. I too was shivevering; some instinct told me this was only a foretaste of a fiercer storm to come.

We had to stay in the cave for nearly an hour, and when at last we returned home we were drenched and exhausted. Darkness was falling, but though the rain had stopped there was still a high wind.

I put Peter away for the night and went in search of my father. The house was deathly quiet, for it was Mary's night out. I switched on the light in the hall and ran upstairs. When I opened the door of his bedroom, I stared in horror at an empty bed. He had gone. By the side of the bed was a bottle; that too was empty.

I ran from room to room, calling his name. He was no-where to be found. I stood in the hall, clutching the banis-ters, cursing myself for betraying my trust. He must have finished the whisky and staggered out to get some more. I should have known, I should have looked to see that he had enough. Now, anything might happen . . .

I went into the drawing-room, and sat there in the dark, with the wind howling round the old house and the thunder muttering behind the hills. I felt very frightened. If my mother had been here she would have done something – her incredible strength would have once again risen to the occasion. She would have turned on the lights, and spoken quiet words of comfort; she would have gone to the kitchen and made some tea; she would have tidied up the bed; she would have created, by the sheer force of her personality, some sort of order out of the chaos.

I rose to my feet; I could not go on sitting there, in the great empty room with the lightning flickering on the walls. I must do something; I must go out and look for him.

From this moment onwards the nightmare darkens, takes a swifter pace, though some of its details are, and always will be, hideously vivid to me. I remember that the light was out in the cloak-room when I went to get a macintosh, and that by mistake I seized one of my father's, which hung round me in grotesque folds and rattled in the wind as I ran up the drive; I remember pausing at the gates, staring about me, wondering whether to go uphill or down. I chose downhill, because that was the district where the town was nearest and the public houses most plentiful. I remember boarding a tram and jumping off at the Clock Tower, and running towards the bright lights of the Queen's.

There I paused, in the darkened archway, and stared at the frosted-glass door, at the legend 'SALOON BAR', listening to the clatter and clink of glasses inside.

I pushed the door open; it was the first time I had ever been in a bar; and even to this day, when I enter one, I seem to see on every door a ghostly tracery of that same frosted glass, with its pattern of fleurs-de-lis. There was a merry crowd inside – mostly sailors and their girls; one of the sailors clutched me by the arm and asked me to have a drink; I pushed him away and hurried round to the other side, pursued by the raucous cries of the barmaids, who indeed had every right to object to my presence. After all, I was only fifteen and a very scarecrow fifteen at that, in my father's macintosh.

He was not there. I went out, on to the next pub, and the next. Again and again I made my breathless entrance, stared at the rows of faces, the blowsy women, the leering sailors, blinked in the fumes of tobacco smoke. In all I believe I went to seven bars; and it was like the seven circles of hell.

Never a sign of him. Worn out, I gave it up. The last tram was just winding up towards the haunted hill. I boarded it. Then minutes later I passed through the gates of our drive. A high wind roared through the trees, and the sky was littered with dirty little clouds, blown hither and thither in lunatic disorder.

I did not go straight indoors. My first thought was of Peter. He would be feeling lonely; he might be frightened by the storm. So I hurried across the courtyard. To my dismay the door of the coach-house was open, and as I stepped inside I saw, in the corner, an empty basket – his little bed. The straw was scattered over the floor, and some old gardening tools, rakes and hoes and brooms, had been wrenched off their hooks, as though somebody had been throwing them at him. Somebody. Of this final monstrosity I will not accuse my father, because I was not there to witness it, but can I be blamed for assuming, in my young tortured mind, so old and so finely tutored in the practice of cruelty, that this was what had actually happened? I was torn, rack-wrenched, between two fierce emotions. The bitter grief that Peter had gone, and that I should never see him again – as indeed, I never did. And the even more bitter hatred that at long last, after an eternity of fifteen years, had crystallized into the compulsion to kill.

.   .   .   .   .

Our laws are wrong.

Some murders, I can attest, and some attempts at murder, are justified. In the Old Testament God sometimes speaks more truly than in the New.

I walked like an automaton, bent on murder, in the wake of my father. I walked into the hall, and switched on all the lights. I remember catching sight of myself in the mirror that hung on the wall just by the entrance; I remember, too, a curiously detached interest in the glaring pallor of my face. I did not know that anybody could go so white.

I stumped upstairs, hands hanging by my side, still in the macintosh; always the automaton. I wasn't crying any more.

Still he eluded me.

Very well. He must be somewhere in the garden. Maybe he had gone to his favourite seat by the lily-pond. It lay on the lower terrace, overshadowed by the branches of ancient trees.

That was where he was; but he had gone a step too far. The terrace was bordered by a steep grass bank that swept down to the lower lawn, and he must have staggered over the edge, for there he lay at the bottom of the slope. I could see him very clearly in the bright moonlight; he lay on his back and was muttering to himself. One extraordinary detail impressed me; his eyeglass was still firmly fixed in his eye, and as he turned his head towards me it glittered.

I looked round to make sure that nobody was about. I had no idea what I was going to do; all I knew was that I must take the life of the thing that lay below. As I turned I noticed, only a few yards away, the big iron roller which we always used on the tennis court. Yes. That would do as well as anything. It was so heavy that it needed a strong man to pull it. If I could send it hurtling down the bank and over his head, it would surely crush him to death. And that, I reflected, might well look like an accident. Only a few weeks ago, in the presence of Mary and my mother, he had caused an hysterical scene because the odd man had left 'the roller' too near the edge of the bank. 'It'll be the death of somebody one of these days,' he had shouted. Well, he had been right. It was about to be the death of *him*.

I walked over to the roller and gave it a tug. It was already on a slight incline, and it moved easily – indeed, all too easily, and I had to dig my heels into the ground to control it. Foot by foot I dragged it across to the edge of the bank, checked it, and swung the handle round till it was pointing at his head. The glittering eyeglass made an easy target. I took one last look at him, then I threw back my head and stared up to the sky. It seemed to be growing lighter; the moon was riding free of the clouds. 'In a moment he will be dead,' I thought. 'But he will not go up there – the sky would vomit him away – he will be sucked down, down into the earth.'

I leant on the handle. The roller began to move, very slowly ... faster. Then it leapt from my hands and charged down the slope. There was a strangled cry, and silence.

But death, that night, did not visit the haunted hill.

Instead, at dawn came the doctor, summoned by a tearful Mary, who had gone out and found him lying there with nothing worse than a broken leg. She had run into my room, where I was lying fully dressed on the bed, staring out of the window, looking down through the trees towards the terrace, half dreading, half hoping, that a black shape would appear and come creeping towards me.

She shook me by the shoulder. 'Master Beverley, there's been a nasty accident. Your father ...' And then she told me what had happened.

In an instant I was in a fit of violent hysteria; laughter took me by the throat, tearing and twisting me; it was like being tortured by some giant invisible jester.

He had conquered. And at that moment I knew that he was indestructible, immortal. Only with reluctance and at the final hour would the grave open to receive him, and even then he would escape from it and his ghost would roam abroad.

He would be with me through life, and beyond life, for ever and ever, amen.

Book Two

Chapter One

Towards the middle of the nineteenth century, the College of Marlborough, in the County of Wiltshire, opened its great iron gates to the sons of the nobility, the clergy and the gentry; and though my father, in my opinion, had no claim to be placed in any of these categories, I passed through those gates shortly before the beginning of the First World War.

I was a tall, shy boy, and, according to some of my contemporaries, I had a habit of constantly glancing over my shoulder, as though I were being followed. I was a youthful example of those lines in 'The Ancient Mariner', which caused Shelley to fall into a swoon when he first heard them . . .

> *Like one that on a lonesome road*
> *Doth walk in fear and dread,*
> *And having once turned round walks on,*
> *And turns no more his head,*
> *Because he knows a frightful fiend*
> *Doth close behind him tread.*

Memory is of all faculties the most arbitrary, hanging the tapestries of the brain with pictures over which we appear to have no control; in memory some of our childhood haunts are bathed in perpetual sunshine, through others there blows an eternal wind; some are lit with a sheen of moonlight, others glimmer in the grey light of a dawn that never changes. The brain, presumably, selects those moments in our lives when experience is most acute, paints the appropriate backcloth, and then – being indolent – compels us to re-enact all our experiences against that same backcloth.

To me, Marlborough is recalled in a setting of everlasting winter and, even more precisely, of everlasting dusk. The trees in the courtyard are always bare, stark as slashes of Indian ink against a sky of slate; always those skies are clamorous with the cries of rooks, blown hither and thither by the wind that sweeps in from the Wiltshire downs. Somewhere, too, a bell is always tolling – in the chapel, or by the gates, or in some distant outbuilding. A cold wind, the sound of bells, the gaunt silhouette of a chapel against a grey sky – that is the backcloth that memory has painted for my schooldays.

Maybe it sounds melancholy. It was – and it was not. In my final term at Marlborough, when I was correcting the proofs of the novel I had scribbled about it during the holidays – a story called *Prelude* – I searched my brain for a sentence that would sum the whole thing up. I found it in a fragment of Edgar Allan Poe. '*I was not indeed ignorant of the flowers nor the vine, but the cypress and the hemlock overshadowed me night and day.*'

The reader may find some preciousness in such a quotation, applied by a very juvenile novelist to a work of autobiographical fiction which, of necessity, was limited to the hazards and humours of a tough public school. But he must remember that when I first walked through those iron gates, I was already a murderer *manqué*. I had already striven to take a human life – albeit clumsily and unsuccessfully; and often, lying awake in the long dormitory at night, I would ponder ways in which I might try to murder again.

But perhaps the reason for this tinge of melancholy that clouded my schooldays was because I already knew too much of evil and because, with my strained and sharpened perceptions, I saw evil where there was none.

Thus, when I was flogged in dormitory, I assumed as a matter of course that the reason for the flogging was to give pleasure to the prefect who administered it. This did not even strike me as unnatural; I accepted it as part of the natural pattern of human behaviour.

Was this so far wrong? Consider this question of flogging, as it was administered in Marlborough College during the days of the First World War. When a new boy arrived at his school House he was allotted a bed in a dormitory sleeping some thirty other boys. In the centre of the long gaunt room, hanging from the ceiling, was a pair of gymnastic rings. On the new boy's first night it was explained to him by the dormitory prefect that he would be required, after four weeks' practice, to perform what was called a 'turnover' on these rings. A 'turnover' is a gymnastic exercise in which the body is slowly elevated by the arms, with the legs pushed out at an angle of ninety degrees, after which the arms are straightened and the body performs a full circle. It is not as difficult as it sounds, but it requires strong muscles and a delicate sense of balance.

What if the new boy failed to perform this exercise? Then, explained the prefect, he would be given ten strokes, in pyjamas, in front of the other thirty boys. I am not suggesting that this was a major tragedy, though even a couple of strokes stinging on the nearly bare flesh, expertly administered, might cause the toughest of men to cry aloud. But I am suggesting that for the prefects the flogging was keenly pleasurable. In the weeks preceding the ordeal they would lie in their beds, discussing among themselves the procedures, and often they would come up to the dormitory before lights out, to watch the clumsy efforts of the frightened boys practising on the rings. Sometimes, while they were watching, they would take out a cane from their lockers, and swing it down on to a pillow, as a foretaste of what the boys had coming to them.

It was always the prettiest boys who were flogged the hardest.

I was not shocked by this; why should I be? I had come to fashion mankind in my father's image; I expected cruelty, and got it. Nor was I shocked by the dirty little stories that were sniggered in the school-room nor the blasphemous images by which they were accompanied; this was very small stuff; and sometimes I used to smile at the thought of what these small braggarts would think if I were to get up and give them a sample of the real thing. I did not use those words myself, partly because my long familiarity with them had dulled their force, but mostly because words, to me, were delicate instruments of delight; they were not as important as music, but they were the next best thing. Which is why, I suppose, the poets who spoke most directly to me, when I began to read poetry at all, were the poets who used words for their sheer music, poets like Swinburne and Tennyson and Francis Thompson and – of course – Poe. When I first discovered that magical incantation 'Ulalume' I neither knew nor cared what it was about. Which was just as well, for it is about nothing at all. All I knew was that it was an exquisitely orchestrated fragment for flutes and muted strings, written with a pen instead of with a piano.

A piano!

It was through the piano that I gained, in my first few terms, some happiness and even distinction. At last I had a music master – a real music master. He was a young man called George Dyson, who was later to reach the highest eminence as a composer and a scholar of music.* On the first occasion that I played to him, things began badly. I was in a state of painful agitation because Dyson only took advanced students, and how could I hope to have reached his standards? I was almost entirely self-taught; I had never had a proper music lesson in my life; I had seldom even played on a proper piano. And now, to be suddenly confronted with this beautiful singing instrument – to find my fingers on a keyboard that did not have to be coaxed or thumped, and my feet touching pedals that produced magical crescendos and diminuendos – it was almost too much. Even

* Sir George Dyson, K.C.V.O., Mus. D. Oxon, Hon. LLD., etc.

a professional pianist, before a concert, must acquaint himself with the timbre, the touch, and the individual 'temperament' of the instrument on which he is going to play.

Besides, what should I play? If only I could have had an hour or two to find my way about the keyboard, with all its promise of exciting eloquence, I might have tried a Chopin nocturne or one of the simple Mozart sonatas – not that any of them is so very simple. I dared not risk it. Suddenly it was as though my father were speaking. 'Play "The Rustle of Spring",' he seemed to be saying. At family tea-parties when I was bidden to perform to our few respectable friends, I was always expected to give a rendering of this vulgar little piece by Christian Sinding whose popularity resides in the fact that it sounds 'difficult' when, in fact, it is extremely easy. So I would play 'The Rustle of Spring' to Lady Opherts and the Misses Oldfield and Sir St Vincent Hammick, who would keep time with their feet and heave sighs when it was over and tell me that I had a beautiful 'touch'. With 'The Rustle of Spring', at least, I would be safe.

I played it.

But Dyson did not tell me that I had a beautiful touch.

Instead he said, abruptly: 'Do you like that stuff?'

'Not very much, sir.'

'Then why do you play it?' He laughed and answered the question for me; he was a kindly man. 'Family tea-parties?'

The explanation was so poignantly accurate that my cheeks began to burn.

'What would you really like to play, if you chose for yourself?'

'I don't know, sir.'

'Chopin?'

'Of course, sir.'

'Such as?'

I did not dare try one of the nocturnes; the piano was so incredibly sensitive that I would make a hash of it. It would have been like trying to drive a racing motor-car when one had never known anything faster than an ancient tractor.

'Could I get to know the piano for a minute, sir?'

'Fire away.'

He strolled over to the window and looked out on to the courtyard. In the distance one of the eternal school bells was tolling – the bell that gave warning that the gates would shortly close. It was pitched to the note of E and it had a sad but pleasing after-echo that trembled into E flat. I struck the chord of E minor and began to play, taking the tempo from the bell and allowing the melody to dictate itself. This was better, for now the piano was singing. The tune had a clear shape and fell naturally into a framework of thirty-two bars. I hoped that I would be able to remember it.

'What was that?'

Dyson had turned round from the window and was staring at me intently.

'Nothing, sir. I was making it up.'

He seemed about to speak. Then he strode over to the piano, pushed me aside, sat down and replayed the piece that I had just invented.

This was, I think, one of the few 'supreme moments' of my long life. In it I lived more intensely than in any ecstatic climax of passion or of prayer. For a few fleeting seconds I was living as I had been born to live; the melancholy theme of 'All I Could Never Be' had been thrust aside; I was actually *being*. A great musician had taken this melody of mine that had drifted so fortuitously through the window with the bell, and was developing it with all the resources of his technique and his art. And I knew, and he knew, that it was beautiful.

The last chord died away.

'Was that what you wanted?'

'Yes, sir.'

'Then write it down.'

'I don't think I could, sir.'

It was lucky that Dyson was an impatient man; I was near to tears and if he had been sympathetic, instead of brusque, I might have lost control of myself. 'What d'you mean, you don't think you *could*? You know what a crotchet is, don't you? You know what a quaver is, don't you? You can find C on the stave, can't you . . . and turn it into C sharp or C flat? Damn it all, man, don't you realize you're a *composer*?'

After a few days I managed to write down the little tune, and a few weeks later it won the first prize at the Annual Speech Day. I played it to a large audience of boys and parents and bishops and generals, and when it was finished the headmaster mounted the stage and announced, in ringing tones, that the college was proud to number among its scholars 'a young Chopin. By name, B. Nichols, of C House.' Prolonged applause. 'I repeat, ladies and gentlemen, a young Chopin. A budding *Chopin!*' The applause swelled louder.

It was a pity that he repeated it. For the applause woke up the reporter of the local newspaper, who realized that he had stumbled upon a 'story'. A few days later the story was picked up by a London newspaper, and I saw my name in print, as a composer, for the first and almost the last time: 'Schoolboy Chopin.'

Which was to lead to a great deal of trouble.

II

The trouble came to a head on the first day of the holidays.

I was met at Torquay station by my father, and as he strode down the platform I noted with the instant extrasensory perception of long practice that he was nearing the end of Stage One. The pace of his walk, the tilt of his grey bowler hat, the angle of his eyeglass, the twirl of his stick – all these signs proclaimed his condition as clearly as if they had been printed on a sheet of paper. The delirium crisis was at least a week behind us, he had suffered his brief period of remorse, and a few days of comparative sanity lay ahead.

'Well . . . well!' he greeted me. 'Quite a celebrity!' As he spoke he flourished the newspaper cutting about the 'School-boy Chopin', which he had been showing to the head porter, whose name – why should one remember these things with such painful clarity?—was Brewer.

Brewer lugged my school trunk on to a barrow and trundled it out to the waiting cab. My father gave him a shilling, holding it out conspicuously, so that everybody could see it. In those days, a shilling was a princely tip. And so we drove off, in the open cab, down the long promenade, past the 'Rock Walk', to the sound of the sea-gulls. So intoxicated was I by the thought of music, the abundance, the omnipresence of music in every breath of the wind, at every moment of the day and the night, that I found myself translating the song of the sea-gulls into a sort of juvenile symphony, with a soaring accompaniment of wood-wind and a deep undersurge of the sea on muted strings. I did not even know the name of the instruments, let alone how their language could be translated on to paper, but I should learn one day. Yes, I should learn. Mr Dyson would teach me. Everything would be all right.

But would it? As we made our way up the hill towards the Haunted House, the shadows began to gather again. The hill was steep; the cab went slowly; the horse was old. To my father I said . . . 'Shall I get out and walk till we get to the top of the hill?'

'What for?'

I murmured something about lightening the load, helping the horse. This was not well received. There was nothing wrong with the horse. Besides, he had paid five shillings for the hire of the cab. We might as well get our money's worth.

Up to the top of the hill, with the horse sweating and the

trunk sliding on the shabby leather cushions, along the tree-lined road, down the steep, winding drive – and then, home.

This 'home' was called Cleave Court. It was the third and last of our Torquay houses, and since it was the scene of the major part of our story and the background for the more violent manifestations of my father's furies, I have let the other houses fade from the picture – as they have indeed largely faded from my memory. There was a spurious grandeur about the very name of 'Cleave Court'. For a century before my father bought it with his rapidly diminishing capital it had been known as 'Cleave', but that was not good enough for him. 'Cleave Court' looked much better on the writing paper, particularly when it was surmounted by the family crest – to which, as far as I am aware, we had no sort of entitlement. This crest was a fox's head over the words *'Spero Meliora'*, and the legend often struck me as very apposite. 'I hope for better things.' I did indeed.

So to Cleave Court we came, and I felt the familiar chill as I stepped into the hall. This was always the coldest part of the house, and it was made colder still by the draughts that even in high summer swept down the broad staircase from the west wing. And how dark it was, with the fake Elizabethan dressers and the rickety gate-leg tables and the sombre wall-paper! From the high walls the bogus ancestors stared down, looking more suspect than ever, and even more sinister, as though they knew that they were in fancy dress, masquerading under false pretences. Their eyes followed me as I walked down the long corridor that led to the billiards-room. 'A sure sign of a good portrait,' my father often said, 'when the eyes of the sitter follow you.' This was the only artistic instruction he ever gave me.

Home again, and my arms round my mother's shoulders, and the familiar sweet scent of eau-de-Cologne, and the instant, unspoken dialogue between us when our eyes met –

telling each other that things were not too bad, and that there was nothing to fear for a day or two.

The storm broke only a few hours later.

III

I had gone into the drawing-room to play. The piano was even more cluttered than usual and an Indian shawl had been spread over it to conceal the stains from a glass of neat whisky which my father had spilt. There were more silver-framed photographs than ever and – worst of all – the stuffed badger had been replaced. I have not previously mentioned this repulsive object. It was a very large badger with a sharp black snout and highly polished feet. Its fur was moulting and it had evil little eyes of bright orange glass. The only reason why it was so prominently displayed was because my father boasted that he had shot it. He had, in fact, bought it for two shillings at an antique shop next to a saloon on the Marine Parade. However, it would have caused another ugly scene if I had removed it. So that was the background against which I made my music.

What should I play to celebrate my homecoming? On such an ancient and arthritic instrument anything that demanded any delicacy of touch or subtlety of pedalling was out of the question, so I chose Bach's Italian Concerto. Mr Dyson had said that it would be within my range. I had hardly struck the first chords – among the most challenging that the master ever wrote – when my father was at the door, with my mother behind him.

'What's that stuff?'

'Bach.'

'Sounds like five-finger exercises.' He lurched into an arm-chair. 'Why don't you play some *real* music?'

This might be my moment of truth. 'That's what I want

to do,' I said, looking him straight in the eyes. 'That's what I want to do. All my life.'

'What d'you mean . . . all your life?'

'I could make a living out of it. When I leave school.'

'Out of *music*? How? Playing in a band?'

'I wouldn't mind playing in a band. It might lead to playing with an orchestra.'

'Playing with an orchestra?' He turned to my mother. 'Who does he think he is? Paderewski?'

I caught my mother's eye, and then I noticed her hands. She was twisting her wedding-ring round her finger, again and again, as though she were chafing at a chain.

'I asked you a question,' repeated my father.

She made a pathetic attempt to smile. 'Well, they did call him a young Chopin.'

'*Who* called him that? A hack reporter!'

'But he was quoting the headmaster.'

'What does *he* know about it?'

'It wasn't only the headmaster. It was Mr Dyson.'

'And who's Mr Dyson? A twopenny music-teacher. Doubt if he makes four hundred a year. Is *that* what you want?'

He was beginning to shout, but he pulled himself together with an effort. After all, the First Stage was not yet over – not quite. The mask was still on, though it was slipping fast. For a few days longer he would be playing the role of the loving father, the sporting aristocrat *manqué*, who was making gallant sacrifices to give his son a gentleman's education.

So he lurched out of his arm-chair and walked over to the piano – quite steadily. He still had admirable control of his legs. And he delivered himself of an amiable little lecture on these lines. 'Music? Pshaw! Forget about it, my boy! You're going to the bar! Only three professions for a gentleman . . . the Church, the Army, and the Law. You're going to be a barrister. You've got the brains. Look at your last report! You're going to Oxford. You'll get a scholarship. No doubt about it. Headmaster said so. But music!' He turned to my mother. 'Agreed?'

My mother said nothing. That was the tragedy of her life, and of mine. She never contradicted; never spoke up. She was bound by the relentless chains of the marriage service.

My father had won again, as he always won. He was quite pleased with himself. Cock-of-the-roost. Master in his own house. All signs of revolt repressed. And – no doubt – the pleasing thought of a bottle of whisky in a drawer upstairs.

'All the same,' he continued magnanimously, 'that's no reason why you shouldn't go on with your lessons. What do we pay for 'em? Two guineas a term, isn't it? Well, it's enough, but we can manage it. Besides – as I was saying to your mother the other day – it's a social asset. When you're called to the bar you'll be asked out to dinner and it'll do you no harm if you can sit down and tickle the ivories.' (He really did use this revolting phrase.) 'But not with that sort of stuff.' (Referring to the Bach.) 'What's that piece old Lady Hammick likes so much? "Rustle of Spring"? Let's see if you remember it.'

So I played 'The Rustle of Spring', feeling that it would be more suitably entitled 'Dirge for December'. My fingers were taut with anger and my eyes were blinded with tears. Through these tears I saw the stuffed badger blinking at me with its evil orange eyes, and beyond the badger the dim figures of my mother and father, against a background of dark brown wall-paper.

But what did it matter? The piano was hideously out of tune. So much the better. The soft pedal was stuck and the loud pedal was erratic, so that the pedestrian harmonies were indefinitely prolonged. Good. This was as it should be. There and then, in this moment of time, in this haunted house, I was being offered the role of a hack and I accepted it. What else was there to do? What *could* I have done?

Again and again, in the long years that were to follow, I have asked myself that question. Maybe, if I had been a ruthless and dedicated musician I should have run away from home that very night, and simply disappeared. But it would not have been easy, on a total capital of fifteen shillings in my pocket, with nowhere to go, nowhere to sleep but the open road, and no friend to offer shelter. All the same, I wish that I had done it. Somehow or other I might have reached London, got a job, found somebody, somewhere – and a piano. Only a piano, and a bare room, and enough to keep body and soul alive.

If this crisis had occurred in the 'seventies I hope and believe that I should have had the courage to become a male prostitute, though I doubt whether I should have been very good in the role. The qualities demanded by the successful prostitute – as history so often reminds us – are as much mental as physical, and though I had the right sort of physique I had not the right sort of mind. Even so, throbbing as I was with music that was being stifled at birth, I might have taken this last desperate step to realize my musical ambitions. And in this day and age, when every schoolboy has been conditioned by all the popular media of publicity to regard homosexuality as part of the accepted order of society, would my conduct have seemed so outrageous? My father's '*crimen horribile*' is no longer a crime at all; as for being '*non nominandum*', it is so frequently discussed, in such interminable detail, that the bogy of the past is rapidly becoming the bore of the present.

But even if there had been no such change in the climate of opinion, I should have been supported by an overwhelming conviction that what I was doing was morally right. I should have endured the ultimate physical humiliations with no shadow of shame or regret. Of what importance was the prostitution of a body compared with the deliberate murder of a talent?

But the crisis did not occur in the seventies; the Wolfenden report and the Permissive Society were fifty years ahead. And even if the social background had not been so dramatically different, there was one other reason why I did not run away – the love that held me to my mother. The authentic genius must have the ruthlessness to reject all ties of sympathy and affection, so maybe I was not the authentic genius. That question, today, is academic. The fact remains that it was beyond my power to leave her. She had my brothers, who in their separate ways were a source of strength and comfort, but I was the closest. We spoke the same language, we heard the same music, and we were tied most closely by the same terror and the same distress.

Besides, something else had happened to add confusion to a story that was already tragically entangled.

There was 'a war on'.

Chapter Two ✧

The Second World War was a bigger and better edition of the first. Such is the general assumption, but it is a view that I have always found difficult to accept. True, the tragedy of 1914 was enacted on a small screen, in furtive greys and blacks, whereas in 1939 it was presented in Glorious Technicolor, with Death in person at the Wurlitzer organ. True again, in the second war millions more were killed; there was an immeasurably greater destruction of property; and the prevailing lunacies, such as anti-Semitism, were far more widely disseminated. Mankind, in short, was brought to the very edge of the cliffs of total annihilation, on which we have been teetering ever since.

And yet, if we agree that all the world's a stage, the story of the first war was written by a more ruthless dramatist, and with a crueller pen. I have already expressed my reasons for holding this opinion, in the foreword to another book, from which the publishers have kindly given me permission to quote.*

> The revulsion from agony, when it was all over, was far less keen after the Second World War than after the First. Perhaps this was due, in part, to the difference between the physical conditions of the combats. The main horror of the First World War was the long-drawn-out torture of the trenches in France, which was enacted on our very doorstep; it was as though the screams of the wounded could be heard across the Channel; the stench of the corpses in No-Man's-Land might have been blowing over the Sussex Downs. To an island population, living in comparative comfort – and they included the intelligent

* *The Sweet and Twenties* by Beverley Nichols. Published by Weidenfeld & Nicolson.

young men, who were still at school – this gave to the tragedy a specially hideous twist; it was as though we were sitting impotent in the stalls watching a body being slowly done to death on a brightly lighted stage.

This particular horror was not present in World War Two. The whole civil population was involved. Our sensitive youth of 1940, bending over his Latin verbs at Eton, was aware that at any moment the sirens might be sounding and hell break loose over his head. As for his mother, reading her morning newspaper in London, the accounts of yesterday's battles abroad seemed less harrowing because she was reading them in a house from which the roof had just been blown off. The world, it is true, was supping on horrors, but we were all sitting at the same table. Because of this, even Hiroshima did not make so lasting an emotional impact as Ypres.

There was another reason why our intelligent young man, who was a schoolboy during the First World War, carried with him this poignant awareness of the physical agonies of war; he was being eloquently reminded of them by a series of brilliant writers who themselves had experienced those agonies. No novel of the fifties had a fraction of the emotional impact of Remarque's All Quiet on the Western Front, which revealed the naked reality of war as vividly as if a bandage had been ripped from an open wound. No poet of the fifties distilled such concentrated bitterness as Siegfried Sassoon, in such a typical poem as 'Blighters'.

'Blighters'

The House is crammed: tier beyond tier they grin
And cackle at the show, while prancing ranks
Of harlots shrill the chorus, drunk with din;
'We're sure the Kaiser loves our dear old Tanks!'

I'd like to see a Tank come down the stalls,
Lurching to rag-time tunes, or 'Home, sweet Home',
And there'd be no more jokes in Music-halls
To mock the riddled corpses round Bapaume.

Siegfried Sassoon would have found plenty of copy in Torquay, in the secluded drawing-rooms where the leisurely succession of 'At Home' days went on its tranquil way.

Seldom did any gleam from the inferno of Flanders flicker across our placid harbours. There were, of course, a few unpleasantnesses, such as the occasion when young Reggie Smythe threw himself off the end of the pier. So good-looking he had been, and the heir to a baronetcy – but obviously a little queer in the head. He had been sent home with shell-shock, and everybody had been anxious to treat him as a hero, but he had obstinately refused to talk about the war. And sometimes, when the old generals were explaining the strategy of the shambles – illustrating their expositions by dotting silver cream-jugs and sugar-bowls over the gleaming table-cloths – young Reggie would begin to laugh, in a high desperate tenor, that suggested a young man being strangled in the mud. It was really quite distressing and perhaps his death – so said the old ladies of Torquay, after they had recovered from the shock of his body being fished out of the water on a boat-hook – had been a 'blessed release'. Not only for him, but for them. That strangled laughter had been so . . . so 'upsetting'.

At this distance of time, if I had to evoke my own adolescent recollection of the First World War I should do so in a phrase of music – the melody of Ivor Novello's 'Keep the Home Fires Burning'. Years later, when Ivor and I were collaborating on a Cochran revue the memory of this pleasant little tune used to haunt me, to the detriment of my own efforts to write popular music. The song was a great favourite with the old ladies of Torquay, who asked for it so frequently that I varied its monotony by improvisation. On one occasion, when the morning newspapers had brought the tidings of a particularly gruesome carnage, I turned it into a funeral march, transposing it into a minor key with a pedal accompaniment in the bass. This was thought to be in very poor 'taste'; as though one were tampering with something sacred. (The tune had, in fact, been played at morning service in our local church, St Mathias in the Wellswood Road.) But perhaps the real reason for the old ladies' partiality to Ivor's song lay in the fact that it soothed their consciences; it made them feel that they were 'doing their bit'. The morale of the 'home front' was just as important as the morale of the battle front, was it not? General Haig himself had said so. Sometimes, indeed, they felt that *their* task was the harder. Nobody would dream of denying that the dear boys 'out there' were 'putting up a wonderful show' but *they*, at least, had excitement to spur them; *they* never had a dull moment. Whereas in Torquay, though of course one was not complaining, there was very little going on. Even the Saturday night symphony concerts at the Pavilion had been discontinued. So please, my dear Beverley, will you play that beautiful song once again, as it should be played, in a major key and a marching lilt? And afterwards, perhaps, some Chopin, while we sit around the fire?

II

My father's reaction to the war was typical. The word 'German' was forbidden in the house; a German was a 'Hun' and as such must be described. This made intelligent conversation about the war even more difficult than in most British households, particularly for my mother. The least vindictive of women, the word 'Hun' came uneasily from her lips, and she was constantly offending him. When she did, he would stick in his eyeglass and stare at her, asking her who these 'German friends of hers' might be? *He* knew no 'Germans'. *He* only knew 'Huns'.

Meanwhile he was actively concerned in contriving some means by which he might give his 'services' to his country. He was – alas – too old to join the Army, too sodden to be sent out to France. But we must all 'do our bit'. With his 'experience', his 'talent for organization', his 'knowledge of men' (he actually employed such phrases) surely there was *something* he could do?

And so, from the Haunted House, a flood of letters was

dispatched to government departments informing them that John Nichols, ex-solicitor of Bristol, was willing, nay eager, to put himself at the disposal of his King and Country. These letters, and the method of their composition, threw a vivid light on the master–slave relationship between him and my mother. He no longer penned his own letters; he had 'too many other things to do'; and so he promoted my mother to the role of secretary. His was the brain, she was the humble instrument to whom he dictated. Apart from that, as he was obliged to admit, his own hand was often too shaky to write a legible script. ('This damned heart of mine's been playing me up again.')

Therefore it fell to her, day after day, to sit at a table taking down the pompous hackneyed words in which he phrased his ludicrous suggestions. She had countless things to do about the shabby rambling house; there was the drawing-room to be turned out, the rug in the morning-room to be repaired, the curtains in the billiards-room to be rehung, and all of the boards of the floors in the various guest-rooms needed restaining – not that we were ever likely to have any guests! Even if she had been able to perform these labours of Hercules, her beloved, neglected garden would still have been calling to her.

But no, there was more important work at hand; these trifling, feminine details could wait, while my father dictated. I can still see his shadow moving round the study, and some of his favourite phrases still echo as clearly as if he were in the next room, for they were repeated *ad nauseam*. Of all these, three words irked me most – '*Having regard to*'. When at a loss for anything else to say, he said '*Having regard to*'. Then again, indeed over and over again – '*Not entirely lacking in*'. This was an ironic way of referring to his own qualifica-tions, which, as we have seen, came under the general head-ings of 'experience', 'organization', and 'knowledge of men'. For hour after hour my mother copied those phrases, in her pretty, delicate script. '*Having regard to the fact that I am not entirely lacking in etc. etc.'* Then, when he could think of no more government departments to pester, she would be rewarded with a patronizing pat on the back, and he would go out for his morning stroll, to 'change the library books' – which meant, of course, a couple of double whiskies at the Queen's. At the door he would usually pause to remind her that the letters she had been taking down were only 'rough copies' and that he would need her to do them again when he had 'polished them up'.

Fortunately for my mother, this particular form of slavery lasted for only a few weeks. True, she continued to take down his letters almost to the day of her death, for with the years his sloth increased, and his shakiness. But the 'war letter' period was short-lived. Nobody, it seemed, needed the services of John Nichols, Esq., ex-solicitor, of Cleave Court, Torquay. The few friends in high places, of whom he was accustomed to boast at our tea-parties, were strangely indifferent to his solicitations.

III

Now it was that the war began to irk my father, to arouse the slumbering beast in him, not that it ever slumbered for long. Seeing all life in the light of his own devouring egotism, he felt that the war was not giving him a fair deal. He was getting nothing out of it, not even a taste of blood.

Here he was, with three strapping sons, and not one of them fighting for King and Country – not one of them even in uniform! It was hard to bear. Life was cheating him, denying him the proper rewards of paternity. How gratifying it would have been to stroll into the Queen's and pass round a photograph of my brother Paul – 'he ought to be a major by now, at his age' – or of my brother Alan – 'six foot two and as strong as a horse!' What touching scenes he could have enacted if one of them had been wounded – how he would have paraded him through the town, and shown himself off! And how full his cup would have been – with whisky – if one of them had actually been killed!

As yet, it was too early in the war for him to hurl his reproaches at myself. Besides, I was doing too well at school for him to use me as a whipping-boy; I was winning rather more than my fair share of prizes and the Chopin episode had not yet begun to rankle in his mind. Even so, he managed to use me as an instrument to torture my mother. Her principal interest in the war, like that of most mothers, was a passionate longing for it to stop before any members of her own family were involved. Though it would not be true to say that she was 'unpatriotic', she was mercifully devoid of the sort of jingoism that was convulsing the smug and narrow society that surrounded us. When Lady Opherts, the Misses Oldfield and the rest of them began to talk at our tea-parties of the wholesale rape of Belgian nuns – though they were too ladylike to use such a word as 'rape' – my mother played no part in the conversation. She took those nuns with a pinch of salt. When war aims in general were discussed her only comment was that she 'did not know what the war was all about'. This, as most contemporary historians will agree, fifty years later, showed her very good sense. Perhaps her essential sanity was most clearly demonstrated in a brief, ironic comment she made at the end of the war, when the wiseacres of Versailles were drawing up the bill which they were to present to Germany, in the fond hope that they could extract the entire cost of four years' destruction. 'We shall never get the money,' she said. This greatly angered my father, who believed everything the papers told him. 'What do *you* know about it?' he stormed. '*Why* shan't we get the money?'

'Because,' replied my mother, 'there is not that amount of money in the world.'

Which, when one comes to think of it, is a fairly accurate summary of Keynes's *Economic Consequences of the Peace*.

Meanwhile my father diverted himself by using me to increase her nervous tension. He would sit in his arm-chair, and his bloodshot eyes would light on a picture of my brother Alan. 'He ought to be in it,' he would mutter. 'Putrid funk.'

'It is not Alan's fault,' my mother would reply, for the hundredth time.

'He's as fit as I am.' Then he would suddenly remember that *he* was not supposed to be at all fit; *he* was not long for this world; *he* had a 'heart'. (We were to hear about this 'heart' for the next thirty years.) So he would shift in his arm-chair and repeat that anyway Alan was a 'putrid funk' and that he deserved to be sent white feathers. These, the younger reader may need reminding, were the tokens of contempt which, during the First World War, the patriotic ladies of England were wont to offer any young man in the street who was not in uniform. They handed them, at random, to consumptives, to foreigners, and to young officers enjoying, in civilian clothes, a brief respite from the hell of Flanders. It takes all sorts to win a war.

Then he would turn his attention to my brother Paul. 'He's as bad,' he would mutter. 'Gallivanting round the world with his putrid bishop.'

'You have no right to say such things,' reproached my mother.

'Shut your mouth.'

'You have no right.'

And she would go over to take up the photograph of Paul, which was the last she had of him. It showed him lying in hospital in an Indian hill station. His body was enclosed in a plaster cast and she wondered whether he would ever walk again.

Even my father could hardly develop the suggestion that Paul, at the moment, would cut an impressive figure at a recruiting station.

So he had to content himself by turning back to me.

142

'Never mind!' His voice would become quite cheerful. 'There's still Master Beverley. He'll be in it all right!'

My mother's face would cloud with distress. 'He's too young.'

'That doesn't matter. The war's going on a long time yet!'

And he would look at me with a gloating smile. 'You'll be in it, won't you, m'young feller m'lad? You'll show them you're made of the same stuff of your poor old father.'

Then he would sink back into his arm-chair, and close his eyes. Maybe life was going to be kind to him, after all. Maybe it was going to give him a long war, and the satisfaction of a blood sacrifice.

IV

Let us take a look at Alan . . . 'the putrid funk'.

Here are three pictures of him. The first, in a silver frame, stands on the drawing-room mantelpiece. It shows a young man in the uniform of a lieutenant in the Gordon Highlanders, holding himself with a swagger, his keen eyes greeting the camera as though he were already facing the enemy. You can almost hear the swish of his kilt. He is the prototype of youthful courage and gallantry.

How Alan ever got himself into this historic regiment, and how he managed his commission, is something of a mystery to me, as it was to all of us. He simply disappeared, in the first weeks of the war, and then reappeared in the uniform of the Gordon Highlanders. A fighter born, who might have been a fine leader of men, he had achieved his great ambition – to join the Army. By doing so, he gave great satisfaction to my father who paraded him proudly before the local inhabitants, on his first and only leave.

There is only one thing wrong about this photograph in the silver frame. It is a fake. A most honourable fake, a forgery contrived with the highest motives, but still a fake. For Alan, in his passionate desire to join the Army, concealed the fact that he was an epileptic. All went well for a few weeks, until one morning he had a seizure on parade, and that was the end of the Gordon Highlanders. Even then, he did not give up. He changed his name, found another regiment, passed another medical board, under the same false pretences. It was all to no avail. His malady, inevitably, was discovered. And that was the end of the Army, for good and all.

This leads us to our second picture of him. The scene is the stage of a provincial theatre. The war is being waged with increasing frenzy. Although manpower is running short, there is as yet no conscription. On the walls of the theatre, next to the placards advertising the weekly play – a touring company of 'The Arcadians' – hang immense recruiting posters showing Lord Kitchener, his eyes blazing behind the world's largest moustache. He is pointing an accusing finger at the passers by, proclaiming, in letters three feet high . . .

YOUR KING AND COUNTRY NEED YOU

It is a sign of the times, and a healthy one, that when this poster was paraded in a nostalgic episode during a recent London revue the audience was convulsed with laughter. If I had been of a younger generation I should have joined in that laughter.

But our eyes were on the stage of the small theatre. Alan stands in the centre of this stage, a young man whose services, one would have thought, Lord Kitchener would have been only too eager to enlist. He is so handsome, so brimming with vitality, that we can hardly be surprised at the cheers that greet him when the curtain falls, nor at the crowd of autograph hunters who gather round him at the stage door. Nor can we be surprised to find among those autograph hunters a sprinkling of the ladies of the White Feather Brigade, handing out their sinister little emblems. Alan receives them with a smile; he is used to that sort of thing by now.

The scene changes again for our third picture, and we are back in the Haunted House. Somewhere in the north of England the touring company of the Arcadians is still trundling around, but Alan is no longer in it. Once again his disease has found him out, not on the parade ground, this time, but behind the footlights. Which was the end of his career on the stage, but not the end of his agony. He is in the throes of it as I recall this scene; he is lying at the top of the stairs, almost naked, writhing, with the spit coming from his mouth. In the meantime my father is spreadeagled at the bottom of the stairs, drunk beyond redemption. My mother, fortunately, is away for the night. This is a crisis with which I must deal alone, and in retrospect it might be classified under the heading of black comedy. Melodrama is perilously near to farce, and at this particular moment, so deeply scored in my memory, even the weather was being melodramatic. There was a violent thunderstorm.

So deeply scored in my memory . . . is that strictly true? I think so. It was ten o'clock. I had been in the drawing-room, trying to play the slow movements of Bach's Italian Concerto. Then the storm blew up over the hills, and with the storm came the lightning, of which I was very frightened and always shall be. For when we were children my father's method of instructing us in the dangers of lightning was to hurry round the house removing all objects that might reflect the flashes, sweeping the silver from the dining-table, covering the mirrors with sheets lest they should attract the vengeance of the heavens, and regaling us with stories of little boys who had been 'struck' and crippled for life in the most terrifying ways, so that their legs were permanently twisted round their necks.

Yes. It *was* ten o'clock, for the chimes were still ringing through the hall. And I *was* playing the Bach – to this day I can remember the intricacies of the fingering. And my father *was* at the bottom of the stairs. And the lightning *was* all through the haunted house.

Then came this cry for help. And I ran up the staircase and Alan was lying there, writhing, with the spit coming out of his mouth. The fit had taken him in his bath.

And yet, this scene emerges finally as a comedy. For as I ran after him, to his bedroom, and tried to catch him as he fell on to the shabby carpet, my one thought was of corks.

I must find a cork, I must find a cork; that was what my mother had told me when this thing happened again, as happen it surely would. Already he had bitten his tongue and the blood was streaming over his chin. I must find a cork to put between his teeth. The lightning flashed through the windows, streaking over the tortured body, tingeing the blood with a sickly hue of green. He was like one possessed by a demon, as indeed he was.

Was this really me? Did I really do these things? Running down the wide staircase, with the lightning flashing on to the bogus portraits, out to the deserted kitchen to find a cork? But why had I come to the kitchen? There seemed to be no cork here. But the whole house must be full of corks, bottles and corks, corks and bottles, hidden in cupboards, in chests of drawers, on the tops of wardrobes. God send me a cork. At last I found one, in an empty bottle that my father had dropped as he staggered to the hall. I was able to force it between Alan's teeth, and wipe away the blood, and bathe his dripping body, and get him to bed. The storm passed, and in the morning the sun was shining again.

In the years ahead, Alan, thank God, was to conquer his malady, to find peace, to marry an enchanting girl, and to raise a family of whom any man might be proud. In escaping from the shadows of the Haunted House he discovered the happiness that was his birthright. And he had his share of life's sunshine.

Chapter Three ~♣~

'You must remember, Nichols, that life is not always a bed of roses. Sometimes there is an *ugly* side to life.'

'Yes, sir.'

'You cannot spend *all* your time dreaming sweet dreams, drifting around in a mist of Chopin, can you?'

'No, sir.'

'Understood?'

'Understood, sir.'

'Good lad.' A hearty slap on my back. The hairy hand remains, pauses, as though the finger were going to creep up the back of my neck.

Then he straightens himself, lifts his chin, and stares straight ahead, with a very fierce expression.

There is a moment's silence.

'And now . . . King Charles!'

I strike the opening bars of this Edwardian chestnut, and he begins to sing.

We are back at school again, and once more we are seated at the piano. Disposed on this instrument are numerous photographs of the same young man – the same not-quite-so-young man – the same near-middle-aged young man.

My housemaster, we will call C.R.P.C., after the fashion of all Marlborough boys, to whom those in authority are sets of initials rather than bodies of men. In these photographs C.R.P.C. is always in the same clothes, shorts and an open shirt, revealing a hairy chest; always in the same posture – knees apart and tightly folded muscular arms; always with the same tense expression, as though he were wondering if his soul was quite as tough as his body would suggest.

I have been promoted. The musical composition prize and the reports of 'The Young Chopin' have had their effect. I am no longer Nichols the dud, who drops every catch at cricket, fumbles every ball at rugger, and sometimes runs in the wrong direction on the football field. I am a celebrity, to be paraded before parents. Apart from that I am useful to C.R.P.C. because somebody has told him that he has a 'voice', and he wants a free accompanist.

He certainly had a 'voice' but it was more fitted to the barrack square than to the concert-room. For this reason it was fortunate that his taste ran to the more robust type of ballad, such as his favourite 'King Charles', which was so robust as to be alarming. 'King Charles . . . King Charles!' he would bawl, facing me from the other side of the piano, so that I saw his wide-open mouth, all the way back to the quivering uvula . . .

> King Charles, King Charles!
> And who's for a toast now?
> King Charles, King Charles!
> And who'll drink the most now?

He roared these questions as though he were really anxious to know the answers.

Apart from 'King Charles' he had a fondness for 'Friend o' Mine'. Older readers may remember this.

> 'When you are happy
> Friend o' mine,
> And all your skies are blue . . .'

He expected me to adapt my facial expression to the changing moods of the lyric, for sometimes, if I did not look bright enough during the 'happy' part, which was written in a major key, he would reproach me for not entering into the spirit of the song.

'The accompanist,' he would say, leaning very close to me, 'must *mould* himself to the artist.'

'Yes, sir.'

'He must follow, but he must also anticipate. He must be ready for the least suggestion.'

I was more than prepared for 'suggestions', but fortunately, they never came. Even so, the whole song was an emotional ordeal; the changes of its 'mood' were so abrupt. The last verse leaps, in a single bar, from major to minor, and the lyric is charged with gloomy forebodings about the day when 'friend o' mine's' skies will no longer be blue but grey . . . and there is even a hint of his premature decease, which demands a number of rallentandos and a plentiful use of the soft pedal.

After the songs it was my turn as a soloist. If I had been allowed to play what I liked I might have enjoyed this part of the entertainment, but we had different tastes. Bach, he informed me, had 'nothing to say' and Beethoven 'went on too long'. He preferred 'moderns', and his favourite of all the 'moderns' was Debussy's 'Cathédrale Engloutie' – a pleasant enough composition, a sort of musical *trompe l'oeil*, but not one of the ten pieces which one would choose if condemned to a desert island. However, I played it well enough, and afterwards, he would be at the piano to explain the meaning of it. 'You see, Nichols? The submerged city, the sea sweeping over the ruined cathedral, the water creeping round the organ, mingling with the music? *That* is the spirit you must try to get.'

'Yes, sir.'

I might have told him that it would have been easier to 'get the spirit' if the piano had not been so sharp and if the soft pedal could have been given a drop of oil. As it was, I was thankful for his interest. This might not be the music for which I yearned, but at least it was music. And at least it was earning a few dividends – an occasional respite from the nets, for example. ('We don't want you to break those fingers of yours, do we, Nichols?')

.   .   .   .   .

I have been reading *Prelude* again, my first novel, which I had not opened for many years. It was a school story written in the summer holiday when I was nearly eighteen years of age. Published during my second term at Oxford, it was generously reviewed. Perhaps the critics were too kind, but after returning to the book there seems no reason to assume a false modesty. It is a remarkable book, and though some of the purple patches have faded into a rather dubious magenta, it is lit by surprising flashes of humour.

The interesting thing about *Prelude*, as far as our story is concerned, is the extent to which it illustrates the author's longing for musical expression. This is a book written by a schoolboy whose fingers reached for a pen because they were denied a keyboard. Our two 'grand' pianos in Cleave Court were by now almost unplayable; the moth had eaten into the felt on the hammers, the wires were rusted, the pedals broken. No pianissimo was possible to achieve – and if I had ever been a pianist I should have most delighted in those moments of mystery and ecstasy when sound trembles into silence. As for fortissimos, they were unthinkable. They would have sounded like a clatter of old tin cans.

So I took to the pen instead of the piano, and the evidence of this ceaseless hunger is on every page. It is even printed on the cover, which bears a replica of three bars of music. The titles I gave to the four parts of the novel were 'Prelude' – 'Modulations' – 'Resolutions' – 'The Last Movement'. Music even enters into the dialogue, sometimes with an effect of comedy that my young mind had not intended. Opening the book at random we find a lively description of a quarrel in a changing-room after a game of football. At the end of this episode I write, of one of the protagonists . . . 'He vanished, humming the Scherzo from the Kreutzer Sonata as he went.' What this was intended to convey, I have long forgotten, but evidently it meant something to me at the time. Rows in changing-rooms, terrors in drawing-rooms, they were all on the keyboard, but my hands were chained.

At the end of the book I killed myself – on paper. Not by my own hand, but in circumstances of outstanding gallantry, on the fields of Flanders. This is the only part of the novel which can now be considered as bad, very bad indeed, and it was chosen for special commendation by the critics.

III

Life went on, the war went on; the roses climbed higher up the walls and the piles of empty whisky bottles would have mounted higher in the cellar, if my mother had not expanded so much energy and ingenuity in disposing of them. ('It was very important,' she often reminded me, 'that the men who collected the dustbins should not *know*.' Even from the possible censures of dustmen my father must be protected!)

Youth went on. My schoolboy complexion, which had once aroused such regrettable emotions in the breast of 'Egie', took on a sturdier tinge. I shaved three times a week in a bath-room reeking of the odours of Glyco-Thymoline. In no spirit of self-pity I ask myself what is 'Youth'? What is it *like*, to be young, not only physically but spiritually, so that one feels that life was intended to be written in a major key? I could go further, and ask . . . 'What is a *home* like? How does it feel to have an open door, through which friends could walk, without uncovering a scene of disaster and disgrace?'

I could even ask the final question . . . 'What are flowers like, flowers on whom no shadow has fallen? How does a man regard a rose with the eye of innocence, without recalling the branches that were broken by a falling body, and the petals that were strewn across the garden path?'

Chapter Four ❧

In the old days of the silent films, the director sometimes indicated the passage of time by showing a calendar with its pages blowing in the wind. Faster and faster it fluttered, in a light that flickered from summer to winter, while in the background one saw trees shedding their leaves, and miraculously sprouting again. I propose to use this device, turning the wind-machine on to the leaves of memory. Blow away Cleave Court, which vanishes in a cloud of debts. Banish the war and its aftermath, draw a blue pencil across thousands of words of unpublished souvenirs. Rearrange the lighting, re-group the leading characters.

If this were the rough draft of an episode in a television series we might begin like this . . .

4 Cambridge Square. A large vicarage in an elegant district of London. Five floors. Don't forget my mother's description of it. 'Yesterday,' she said, 'I walked up the staircases from the cellars to the attics. There were a hundred steps. I counted them.' Don't forget that she said this with a strange sort of pride, as though she were consoled by the fact that she was still living in a great house. Don't forget the flush on her face when she said it. And her breathlessness. Don't forget the doctor's warning.

Keep cameras on 4 Cambridge Square; come closer. All the old props from the previous episodes are reassembled. Everything has been transported from the Haunted House. The bogus family portraits still hang on the staircase. The Collard and Collard grand piano still glowers in the drawing-room. The Broadwood, what is left of it, has been banished to the cellar. The stuffed badger still stares into space with its beady eyes of orange glass.

And the tea-parties still go on. The Torquay ladies are

regathered, under different names, and in the costumes of the twenties, but essentially they are the same people, as though they were members of a touring company in a revival of a successful play. Even their lines have an uncanny echo of the past. My mother is saying . . . 'I am so sorry my husband could not be here to meet you. But . . . but his heart is not too good at the moment.' When she has told her sad little fib she glances nervously around her, studying the faces of her guests, wondering whether they believe her. Sometimes her eyes stray towards the ceiling, for his bedroom is directly above, and the sound of a heavy body crashing to the floor might arouse their suspicions.

II

We left the Haunted House and came to London for a number of reasons, but the principal reason was financial. My father's small capital had been shrinking year by year. Apart from all that was spent on drink, there was a perpetual outlay on doctor's bills and 'cures', which only seemed to make him worse. When my brother Alan married and my brother Paul was given this fashionable London living, surely it would be sensible for my parents to join him?

They would provide the furniture – and a great deal of furniture there would have to be. My mother would keep house and supervise the servants. (Yes, we again had servants!) As for my father, one could but hope.

To me the whole thing seemed madness, and my sense of the insanity of it all was sharpened by the fact that I had now grown up, and was making my way in life, and could view our household with the detachment of a young man of the world.

Perhaps we have turned the pages of our calendar too fast. Perhaps I should have mentioned that while time has been flying I have been making a name for myself, first at Oxford and then in Fleet Street. I have written a couple of best-sellers and I am moving in circles very different from those to which I, or any other members of our family, have been accustomed. I mention these facts merely to stress the sharpness of the contrast between the life of the outside world and the life of the Haunted House – for that was what the vicarage became, as soon as my father stepped over the threshold. In Torquay I had come to accept our fantastic background as a normal state of affairs, but in the London of the twenties, with money in my pocket, and a sheaf of flattering invitation cards on the chimney-piece of my flat, things began to look rather different.

To have luncheon in Grosvenor Square with Lady Cunard, to listen to Mr Winston Churchill perorating as he sniffed the balloon of brandy in his chubby hands, to leave the house to the echo of laughter, to buy a bunch of white roses from the little shop in South Audley Street, to take a taxi to Cambridge Square – in such moments were the ingredients of happiness. I loved my mother very much; the white roses were sweetly scented; and – as always – she took more pleasure in them because she knew that they were expensive. She would ask how much they cost, and smile, and shake her head, and say to me that I should not have wasted my money. Had I really met Mr Churchill? Was Lady Cunard as pretty as her pictures? What had we had for luncheon? Sometimes, because she found a fleeting, vicarious delight in the stories of these small social triumphs, I made them more impressive than they really were. On the few occasions when I went to royal parties I invented conversations with the Queen. Had Her Majesty really said that? Had she really read my books? Yes, I lied, she had. I do not regret those lies.

But only too often the stories could not be told. Always, standing on the doorstep of Cambridge Square, clutching the flowers, waiting for the bell to be answered, the familiar black magic began to work. My stomach sank. The laughter of Grosvenor Square echoed into a far distance, the smiling faces of the luncheon guests became remote and unreal, I was back among the old fears and horrors, waiting to learn what was on the other side of the door. Who would open it? The new housemaid, or would she have gone, like all the others? Who? A doctor? A policeman? Or would I have to force it open myself? If I did . . . what then? What would be there? Something gross and hideous and insensate lying at the foot of the staircase?

All this was in sharp contrast to the gaiety of Grosvenor Square, with its white and gold salons, leading from one to another, under a sparkle of chandeliers. Lady Cunard's house held few objects of importance; her 'best' pictures were by Marie Laurencin, which is not saying much, and her furniture, in the style of Louis Seize, was suspect. It was all rather like the Ritz, and in spite of the sentimental memoirs which have since been composed in her honour, her sharp little mind, *au fond* was that of a brilliant social hôtelier. But at least she was alive; and she enlivened all those who came within her circle. As her guests walked down the great staircase they seemed to walk to the sound of music, and there was always the saving grace of laughter.

Laughter! Perhaps I can best illuminate the immense distances which divided our family from the rest of the world – (so that Grosvenor Square seemed as remote from Cambridge Square as the mountains of the moon) – by recalling the quality of my father's humour. His idea of a joke was to leave his fly-buttons undone. When he was in a specially amiable frame of mind – this was in Stage One – he would retire to his bedroom, gargle with Glyco-Thymoline, undo three fly-buttons, pull out an inch of his shirt, and then slowly descend the staircase, assuming, in the meanwhile, an expression of unawareness. At this delicate comedy we were supposed to laugh, and we did. We laughed for the sake of our mother; if we had not laughed he would have revenged himself on her, with one of the many weapons of cruelty with which his mental arsenal was so well equipped.

She laughed too, forcing her little wrinkled face into a

smile. One of the few occasions when she was unable to laugh was after a dinner on Christmas Eve, when he told a story of particular obscenity which involved undoing his fly-buttons, thrusting his hand into his trousers, protruding his thumb through the aperture, and wagging it about to simulate a penis. Even then, when he had retired to his bedroom, enraged by our failure to appreciate his little pleasantry, her only comment was . . . 'You mustn't be angry. Please try not to feel like that about him. It's not him.'

III

But who *was* 'him'? Who was this man?

In asking this question, and in endeavouring to answer it, we may perhaps be able to throw light on some very obscure recesses of the human spirit, and to justify the portrayal of a character of such darkness that he would scarcely be credible in fiction, let alone in fact.

The operative word is 'darkness'. A word which goes with nothingness and emptiness and utter loneliness. I do indeed believe – although it has taken me a lifetime to reach this conclusion – that my father was possessed by an evil spirit. Although the phrase is melodramatic it is the only one that fits the facts. I believe that my real father was destroyed by drink, that his true personality was thereby expelled, and that nothing was left but an appalling vacuum which had to be filled. Here we are studying a classic and irrefutable example of a man possessed. We saw evidence of this possession on the first page of this book, when he lay on the floor of the dining-room. Presumably the process had been going on for some time; a man does not surrender his soul over-night. Presumably again, in the seven years which had preceded this denouement, my brother Paul may have had glimpses of him as he once was, which would explain why Paul still contrived, through all the ensuing tragedy, to curb his mounting angers, and to retain, however superficially, a conventional father-and-son relationship. I never had these glimpses. My life began with a personal introduction to the devil. The 'him' whom my mother married, the 'him' whom Paul may have been able to remember, in the days of his childhood, was a stranger to me. I never met 'him'. I met only the devil inside him.

Here are some questions for a psychological Sherlock Holmes. How is it that although my physical father emerges with clarity in these recollections, he does not emerge at all, as a four-square figure of a man? He keeps his secrets, hides his tastes, his hobbies, his ardours and his appetites – all except the ceaseless appetite for drink. It is as though, inside the physical husk, there had been nobody there. Suppose that our psychological Holmes were to ask the sort of questions that he would put on the psychiatric couch, he would elicit a series of blanks.

What *interested* my father? I have no idea. In his youth he had been a brilliant lawyer; and he must have been a shrewd judge of men, with a good financial brain, for he had made enough money by his own efforts to retire while still in his thirties. But he never recalled the past and seldom expressed any opinion about the present. Politics he ignored, personalities aroused in him neither approval nor disapproval. Beyond the stagnant backwaters of Torquay history was being remoulded and a panorama of painful excitement was unfolding. He seemed quite unconscious of this. His sole reaction to the First World War was expressed in the single word 'Hun'; when he had said that, he had said all there was to say.

Was he drawn, even momentarily, in times of fear or crisis, to the things of the spirit? No. He never went to church, never opened a bible, never – even in maudlin repentance – fell on his knees to say a prayer.

Did he seek any diversion in the arts? No. He never went to the theatre, never attended a concert. Quite literally, never. He never even entered the doors of a cinema. When my mother and I trudged over the Torquay hills to visit the 'Electric Palace' and seek escape in the early melodramas of Mary Pickford, he never accompanied us. He stayed in his armchair, a nemo staring into nothingness. To suggest that this fits any of the accepted definitions of insanity would be absurd, but 'nothings' add up, particularly on the psychiatrist's couch.

What did he read, apart from the newspapers? I could not tell you. Once a week he 'changed the books' at the library, but what books were they, and what did he think of them? Nobody knows. What did he like to eat? Mutton, beef, fish, chops – sweet things, sour things? I can give no answer. Year after year I sat at his table, and I could measure to the fraction of an inch his alcoholic intake by the manner in which he carved a chicken. But whether he liked it, disliked it, or was indifferent to it, I could not say. It was a husk of a man at the head of the table, but it was not an empty husk. There was something inside, somebody inside – still watching, still active, still ready to strike. This 'somebody' had brought me into the world. But it was not my father.

The final question . . . what did he love? Whom did he love? When, and where, and how was the love expressed? Here the negatives rise to a crescendo, like the background music in the echo chamber of a recording studio – echo upon echo, stretching to eternity in a hall of musical mirrors, nothing meeting nothing, inanity whispering to inanity. Once, no doubt, my father had loved, but by the time I met him my father had gone. The man I tried to murder was not my father, it was the spirit inside him. And love, to this spirit, was a stranger and an enemy.

It is very important, if only for the sake of my own conscience, that this theory should be understood, and accepted, or at least that the reader should credit me with having accepted it, even if I only did so in my subconscious mind. To plot the murder of one's father is not a pleasurable exercise, nor is it lightly undertaken; and to confess one's regret that the attempt was unsuccessful must seem outrageous to the normal man, accustomed to dealing with other normal men. I can understand this reaction, and even sympathize with it; but he must remember that the writer of these words never has been, and in no conceivable circumstances could have been, a 'normal' man, as far as his father was concerned. From the age of six I was confronted with violence and ugliness in its most naked form, and my reaction to it was all the more extreme because by nature I was gentle, and almost morbidly sensitive, responding to the pianissimos of life with as painful an intensity as most men respond to the fortissimos. There we go again! As always the solution must be found in music, and if things had been different, that is how my answer might have been given. On the keyboard I might have thrown violence against violence in a crash of chords and sought the final answer, the ultimate solution, in a melodic line. Things were not different; they were as I have described them. The answer was not given, the music was not made, or even attempted.

Before this book is finished, I hope to be able to produce evidence which will confirm the theory of my father's possession by an evil spirit. Meanwhile, for those who may find this too facile an explanation, I may be able to give more weight to this difficult thesis – or at least more colour, by suggesting that one of the contributing factors to his corruption lay in my mother's nature, in her own shining goodness. Sometimes I have thought that the gods created her, in a gesture of supreme irony, for the special purpose of encompassing his destruction, and her own.

From the general to the particular. When my mother spoke her wedding vows she was sealing her death warrant. The words of the service, to her, were like a piece of music to which the whole rhythm of her future life must be attuned. '*To have and to hold, from this day forward, for better for worse for richer for poorer, in sickness and in health, to love, cherish and obey.*'

Great literature, great music, but – in some circumstances – great nonsense. There are situations in life when loyalty is akin to lunacy. One of the four cardinal principles of the Oxford Group is 'Absolute Unselfishness'. It sounds admirable, and those who practise it are doubtless convinced that it is one of the rungs on the ladder that leads to heaven. In my mother's case, it was one of the stepping stones to hell, not only for her but for all the rest of us.

If her memory were not so dear I would suggest that this Absolute Unselfishness crystallized, as the years went by, into Absolute Obstinacy. Well, I have said it, and will let it stand because it is true. She was incredibly obstinate, not only about my father, but about everything whatsoever in the conduct of her life. She had to be; if she had surrendered in small causes she would have surrendered in great ones; and that would have been the beginning of the end. The whole façade would have collapsed. But she never gave in, and the end, alas, never came.

Here is one example which may bring some light relief. Flicking over the pages of our calendar to the early thirties I must mention that my own personal success has accelerated. I have bought a cottage in the country and – in a few ecstatic weeks of freedom – written a book called *Down the Garden Path* which has caught the popular fancy. I am surrounded by all the apparatus of successful authorship – a house in London, a cottage in the country, servants, secretaries, gardeners, the lot.

The cottage was in a village called Glatton, in a quiet corner of Huntingdonshire, and from time to time I was able to take my mother there for a few days of peace. Of course, my father had to come too, which was regrettable, but at least, as long as he was in my house, under my supervision, he was obliged to behave himself. He realized that there was murder in my heart – not merely the will to murder but the capacity and temperament to murder – and he was frightened. We maintained the conventions but some-

160

times, when he saw me watching him, he got the death message. Whereupon he screwed in his monocle, as a sort of optical self-defence, and while he did so, his fingers trembled. This trembling, this increasing 'shakiness', as he described it, gave me moments of pleasure, though I should have preferred paralysis – the total paralysis of the criminally insane. Still, it was comforting to know that his foundations were being undermined.

The week-ends began light-heartedly; they were an un-qualified success, and every time I drove my mother back to London she looked ten years younger. But gradually – so tortured was she by years of fear and apprehension – she began to complicate every visit by a clutter of tiresome im-pediments. The vicar might call, so she must have an extra dress. The wind might turn chilly, and my father would need a change of underwear. Every possible misfortune was anti-cipated, so that instead of driving into the country we had to spend half an hour loading up the car. By the time we had finished she had worn herself out, and we were usually late for luncheon.

One week in June matters came to a head. The morning was bland and golden, the sort of day when one would wel-come the shade of the old apple trees. But when I entered the hall of the Haunted House the clutter of luggage was even greater than usual. There were three suit-cases, a large bundle tied up in a rug, a couple of sponge-bags, two umbrellas, and a packet of sandwiches wrapped in grease-proof paper, to sustain us if we began to faint from hunger on the journey, which took a whole hour and a half. All this has been assembled at the cost of considerable fatigue, and most of the objects, needless to say, were for my father's use.

My patience began to wear thin; this was carrying eccen-tricity too far. The dialogue went something like this:

'My darling Mother, we are not going on an arctic expe-dition. Why the rugs?'

'I thought he might like to sit in the garden.'

'If he wants to sit in the garden we can wrap him up in a blanket. And why the umbrellas? And what is in all those suitcases?'

She began to murmur about his shirts and his socks and his boots, in case he got his feet wet – never of course a word about herself – and from the way her fingers were twisting together I realized that I had spoken too impatiently, and upset her. It wasn't a case of a temperamental woman taking offence about a trifle; it was simply that she had been obliged to erect certain defences around her, like a hunted animal, that she had tracked out certain paths through the jungle of her life, and that she dared not stray from those paths.

'Never mind,' I said. 'I was only wondering whether I can get them all into the car.'

At that moment I made up my mind that on our next week-end there would be none of this nonsense. We would play it my way. When we returned to London I went on a shopping expedition.

I began at Liberty's, the celebrated establishment in Regent Street. Liberty's has never been a resort of the bright young people, but this is a shop where one can always find lovely fabrics, with a quiet, ageless elegance. So, at least, I thought, peering through the plate glass, with the sound of the buses roaring in the background. Dim velvets and cloudy tweeds. 'Had I heaven's embroidered cloths.'

I went in, and bought a collection of suitably embroidered cloths. Two coats and skirts in a material which, the young woman behind the counter assured me, would 'last for ever'. I didn't want it to last for ever. Just for one happy week-end. Then I took a taxi to Moss Brothers in Covent Garden, where I bought two Norfolk jackets and three pairs of trousers 'suited to a country gentleman'. After which, keeping the taxi for an exorbitant bribe, I went slightly mad. I bought shoes and socks and stockings and razor blades and scarves and handkerchiefs and aspirin and tooth paste and Eno's

Fruit Salts. I bought dressing-gowns and night-dresses and galoshes, and a glittering collection of scents and soaps and bath salts from Mr Floris in Jermyn Street. At the end of the day I motored up to the cottage and hung the things in cupboards, folded them away in drawers and spread them out on shelves.

I walked round the rooms in the dying summer dusk, feeling very happy, luxuriating in the sort of emotions which Arnold Bennett sometimes expressed so poignantly in his novels of the Five Towns. Very obvious emotions. The young man who had made good – the glint of luxury against a background of hardship – the joy of sharing that luxury with somebody one loved. When I went to bed that night I was wafted away on an Arnold Bennett dream. I could see my mother standing in front of the looking-glass, trying on all these pretty things, patting her hair, laughing, putting scent behind her ears.

But it was not to be like that.

When the moment came, two weeks later, when she opened the bedroom door, and saw all the things spread before her, she was frightened. She stared round her in bewilderment. I can't remember all the details of this tragic farce, which began as Arnold Bennett and ended as Dostoevsky. All I remember is the shadow of fear on her face. The parade of luxury was too much; it was like spreading a banquet before a starving child. She could not accept it, because through the long years she had schooled and disciplined herself never to accept *anything*.

The dresses were never worn; the stoppers of the scent-bottles were never unscrewed; the galoshes gathered dust on the floors of the ancient cupboards. The underwear that should have covered the gross body of my father was re-packed, and returned to the Haunted House. Little by little, every item that I had bought on that delirious afternoon was gathered up, parcelled, and taken back to 4 Cambridge Square.

The week-ends reverted to normal, or what she regarded as normal. The clutter of objects accumulated, the bundles multiplied, to such an extent that when the boot of the car had been loaded to capacity the luggage over-flowed on to the back seat. I said nothing because there was nothing to be said. Nobody could penetrate the shell of her defensive obstinacy and few people, I imagine, could have even begun to understand it. But I understood it and sometimes, when I was loading up the car, I felt that all this meaningless impedimenta were symbolical of her own burden. They were part of the defences which she had erected against the slings and arrows of a particularly outrageous fortune.

Chapter Five ❧

The occasion of the third attempt to murder my father can be precisely dated. It was shortly before eleven o'clock on the night of Saturday, March 31st, 1929. This is not a date that I am likely to forget.

Somewhere on the shelves of the second-hand booksellers there may linger a few copies of a book called *Failures*, a collection of my early plays, published in the autumn of 1933. There were three of them, and though they were produced with distinction, and not unkindly received by the critics, none ran for more than a few weeks, and nobody made any money out of them. Hence the title.

The first of these plays was called *The Stag*, and it was exactly forty-eight hours before the curtain rose on the last act of this play, before a crowded audience at the Globe Theatre, that I was busying myself with the contrivance of my father's death.

In the career of an author of versatility the production of his first play is as memorable as any event with which life will ever present him. The weeks of rehearsal were among the most exciting I have ever spent, and by a fortunate chance my father's alcoholic graph ensured that he would be in one of his 'safe' periods at the end of the month, so that he would be able to go to the premiere without any danger of disaster. The reader may recall that for many years we had been able to predict his conduct with reasonable certainty. The rhythm of his life was so firmly established that we adapted our own lives to its tempo.

He was at the end of Stage Four – the delirium stage – on Monday, March 26th. This, as I observed to my mother, hanging up my coat in the hall of the Haunted House at the end of a long day's rehearsal, was most propitious. Yes, she agreed – and it is a sign of our lunatic existence that she said it with no irony – nothing could have been more fortunate. She counted on her fingers. Yes. It meant that on Wednesday, March 28th, he would be up and about again. And that on the following Monday, April 2nd, the day of the first night, he would be right in the middle of his 'good' period.

Then she said this fatal thing. 'Do you think he might go up to the cottage for a few days? To . . . to recuperate?'

'By himself?'

'It might be better if he went alone, just for once. Besides, he'll have the Watsons to look after him.'

The Watsons were a couple whom I had engaged a few weeks before. They had settled down very well. Mrs Watson was an adequate cook and her husband was a competent rough gardener. More important, as far as the present circumstances were concerned, he was a tough ex-Guardsman, who would be able to deal with any emergency requiring physical force.

Although the conception was revolutionary, I accepted it. On the morning of Wednesday, March 28th, my father, with a great deal of trembling and fussing and polishing of his eyeglass, was lumbered into a hired motor-car, and set off for the rural delights of Huntingdonshire.

Had he only known it, he was driving very near to his death.

II

Time. Late afternoon of Saturday, March 31st, 1929.

Scene. The stage of the Globe Theatre, Shaftesbury Avenue, London.

Characters. The cast of *The Stag*, a play in three acts by Beverley Nichols. Many of these characters are still very much alive. Raymond Massey, for example, who is starring in London as I write these words. And Adrianne Allen, an enchanting actress who sat by the side of Sir Noël Coward at the banquet given in honour of his seventieth birthday. I was present on this emotional occasion and after dinner I reminded her of that final rehearsal. Without hesitation she went into a scene from *The Stag* and delivered the passionate speech which marked her exit. So perhaps the dialogue had not been so feeble after all. However, Adrianne always had a remarkable memory, and never fluffed her lines.

Raymond comes up to me and says, 'Beverley, I think we've got a hit.' Adrianne draws me aside to ask about the colour of a scarf she wants to wear for her entrance in Act One. I tell her she's so pretty that it doesn't matter. Many other faces drift from the past, but they are growing dim. What remains, with piercing and painful clarity, is the recollection of my own emotions as I left the stage. I felt that life was enormously worth living; that I had everything that anybody could want – youth, health, talent, money, friends. There was no cloud in the sky, except, of course, the cloud that was always there. And even in the case of my father, I enjoyed an interlude of irrational optimism. Perhaps at long last he would pull himself together. Perhaps somebody would invent a cure. Perhaps the cottage would work on him the miracle that it always worked on myself. He would have had several nights of tranquillity, the Watsons would have looked after him kindly; he would have woken to the song of the birds and the early daffodils would have greeted him through the lattice windows.

With these thoughts I found comfort as I headed for the Great North Road. If I drove fast I should be in time to 'make the tour' – to walk down the paths, bending low over every bed, alert for the signs and tokens of spring. Of all the pleasures that life has offered, this has been the keenest – returning to a garden that one loves, finding out what has happened while one has been away – how many buds have broken, how many green spears have thrust through the expectant earth. Even in the depths of winter I have gone out

167

in the small hours of the morning with a lighted torch, to scrape away the snow from some distant corner, in the hope of finding a glint of early gold.

Dusk was falling when I turned into the lane leading to the cottage and, as always, there was a sense of leaving the cares of life behind, of stepping into a secret world – a world where a hush lay over the meadows, like the mists that drifted from the wide meandering streams, where the ancient willows spoke in whispers. Now came the familiar bend in the road, the glimpse of a thatched roof, the sudden view of white walls sturdily timbered. If I had to choose the happiest moment in my life I should take this moment. Half past five, or thereabouts, on the evening of March 31st, 1929. Behind me the sweet smell of success, all around me, peace, ahead of me the chance of a miracle – the chance that I might meet the man who was my father, actually *meet* him as a father. What would he be like? If it came to that, what would it be like to have a father at all?

The answer was not long in coming.

III

Something was wrong. The cottage was not welcoming me. There were no lights in the windows; the door was not opened by a beaming housekeeper. The cottage was hostile, possessed by an evil spirit. This was no matter of imagination; it was the communication of a psychic fact. I knew.

I leant back in the car, noting with the acumen of a trained reporter the familiar spasms and contractions in my stomach. So we were home again – home, sweet home. Home to the refuge that I had built so painfully, and tried to make so beautiful.

I drove the car into the wooden garage. Yes, there was something very wrong. A pile of peat lay in a corner, carelessly spilt over an oily floor. Stacked against the wall was a bundle of shrubs, their roots exposed and dry. Watson would never have let this happen. As I closed the doors and walked round to the front entrance I noticed that no smoke was coming from the chimneys.

I opened the door. The cottage was silent, with the curious acid silence that lingers in the wake of a violent quarrel. No lamps were lit, but there was enough light to see a sheet of paper glimmering on the old oak table in the hall. I took it up and read it by the light of a torch – the same torch that had been designed for a happier purpose. It was a letter from the Watsons, informing me that my father's behaviour had been so monstrous that they could no longer stay in the house, that they had been obliged to give immediate notice, that they had left their keys at the village post office, and that though they regretted being forced to take such a drastic step, they were sure that I would 'understand'.

Of course I 'understood'. They had been forced to endure for three days the society of a man whom I had suffered for thirty years. It was more than 'understandable' that he had been too much for them. Meanwhile, I stood there alone with something waiting in the next room. Well . . . one had been through it all before. I kept the torch alight, and walked in.

He was lying in a heap by the empty grate. His fly-buttons were undone; he had been sick on his waistcoat, and the room was filled with a most unpleasant odour. I was so accustomed to this sort of situation that these details hardly seemed important; it would be merely a question of routine – doing-up the fly-buttons, wiping-up the vomit, rinsing-out of the clothes under the tap. And all the rest of it.

But what suddenly gave a touch of drama to these familiar chores was the sight of a shattered ornament lying in his hand. This was a small china figure on which I had set particular store – the figure of a shepherdess with rosy cheeks, whom I had discovered walled up in a secret cabinet some months before. She was a person of great sweetness and distinction, and I had planned to write a story about her. Now she lay shattered, with his hairy fingers round her neck. It was a small consolation that in falling, a fragment of china had cut into his wrist, so that his dark blood oozed on to the coconut matting.

Home sweet home. I walked over to the window and looked out. There would still be time to 'make the tour'.

IV

Included in my abundant literary output over the years are a number of detective novels, and I sometimes wonder whether they may have gained authenticity from the fact that they were composed by a man who has actually planned a murder in cold blood.

My first thought was that I might leave him there to die. The fire was out; for several hours he would be unable to hoist himself off the coconut matting; and in the meantime the windows could be opened to let in the cold. (It was growing colder every minute. There was snow in the air.) I could wrench off his jacket and tug off his shoes and force another glass of whisky down his throat, so that he would stay there long enough to freeze to death.

But would it be cold enough? And *would* he die? Might it not be necessary to call in a doctor? Might he not recover, and the whole hideous cycle begin again? Might I not be faced with some difficult problems about why I had delayed seeking medical assistance?

All these questions I pondered while standing over him, shivering, hungry, and very much alone (still remembering my ludicrous ideal of 'meeting my father', an hour ago).

No, I decided, it would not be cold enough. I must get him outside, and keep him there. This meant giving him a double dose of the sleeping pills which my mother had packed for him. They had been prescribed by the latest in the endless succession of his doctors, and he had been warned that in no circumstances must he combine them with alcohol. So much the better. Nobody could prove that he had not taken them himself. I went upstairs, and found them in his sponge-bag, which he had not troubled to open since his arrival. Then I came down and thrust them into his mouth, under the damp black moustache.

As I started to tug him across the floor, one of his eyes opened, and blinked. It reminded me of the eye of an octopus. (Many years later, in a book written, ironically enough, for children, I was to use the eye of an octopus as an instrument of terror.) But the going was hard; it was like dragging a ton of bricks. He weighed seventeen stone and was proud of it. He gloated in his stomach and puffed out his belly on social occasions; obesity, to him, was synonymous with bonhomie.

I dragged this seventeen stone of flesh through the french windows, into the night. His close-cropped head bumped on the kerb of the porch, and as it did so, the octopus eye opened again for a moment. There was life in the old boy yet. Where to deposit him? Not too far. There would be footprints to explain. And many accusing pointers, written in mud and slush, for now it had begun to snow in earnest. The best place would be just outside the window, among the tangled branches of an old rose-bush. They would lacerate his face, and if there were any odd blood-stains to be accounted for, they would confuse the issue.

A few last heaves and tugs and seventeen stone of paternity was deposited in a prickly shrub, with the snow coming down. No octopus eye, this time. Not a sound. Not a movement.

Then I went into my study, lit the fire, sat down at the piano, and set it all to music. It came out as a sort of furious and disjointed étude, and because I had been denied the opportunity to learn the elementary grammar of composition, it was a thing of shreds and tatters, with sharps where there should have been flats, with rests in the wrong places, and quavers where there should have been semi-quavers. I had an aching desire for musical relief . . . it was all there, in my mind, in my heart, in my soul. But He had tied my fingers and broken, or almost broken, my spirit. But not quite. The hours went by and at last the first draft of the piece was finished. It was rough and amateurish but some of the pain and the passion came through. Which is why I shall publish it at the end of this book; some pianist with the necessary technique may care to study it, if only as a musical curiosity.

By now it was past midnight. The fire had died in the grate, and in my heart. But I had said my say, through the only medium in which I was qualified to say it, and I was no longer cold. I closed the piano, and prepared to go outside.

And then – there was a crash and a splintering of wood, and he fell into the room, covered with snow, with blood streaming down his face.

V

Rasputin.

That was the instant literary analogy. The evil monk, battered, axed, poisoned, frozen, but indestructible. I had not battered my father, not axed him – though had such an instrument been available, the last tensions might have broken and the last gesture been made. I had only used the opiates and the snow, and left the rest to nature and – if it does not sound too bizarre – to God.

But he was indestructible. Come hell and high water he would survive. Twisting and turning on the coconut matting he seemed to grow larger and larger and the shadows from his threshing arms were darkening the ceiling.

The rest of this domestic interlude may read as an anti-climax. Over the years, as we may recall, I had been obliged to create an elaborate technique for dealing with this sort of crisis. The inert body to be hoisted to a place of seclusion, the towels and the basin to be fetched, most important of all, the final crucial dose of alcohol to be thrust down the throat in order to minimize the effects of the inevitable delirium.

In the manner of a hospital nurse, dealing with an awkward case in an emergency ward, I proceeded to perform these duties, and at last I got him upstairs, and guided him to bed where he lay staring at the ceiling, both octopus eyes wide open and rolling round as though they were rotating in the face of some monstrous doll. There was not much time to lose; delirium was almost upon him and he must have his corrective tumbler full of whisky. (This is the accepted treatment when no physical restraint is available.) He managed to swallow the whisky, closed his eyes, and began to twitch, but not too violently. I had timed it pretty well.

Then I hurried round the room, removing anything breakable, took away his shoes and emptied his pockets of money, in case he managed to smash down the door and get outside. The last thing I took was the watch from his waistcoat – a heavy gold Victorian ornament which chimed the hours and the quarters, very sweetly, when you pressed a lever on its side. I pressed it now, and the chimes tinkled airily through the room, in delicate sharps and trebles, mingling with the grunts and groans that were coming from the bed. I remember thinking that this moment might serve as a musical paraphrase of my own life, as it has been, as it was, and as it seemed likely to be – the bitter-sweet threnody of a treble that was forever drowned by the uproar of a discordant bass.

I will pass over the next thirty-six hours, which were occupied by the all-too familiar routine of 'pulling himself together'. I had to work more swiftly than usual, compressing into a short period a therapy that normally required four days. It is enough to say that by Monday morning he was sufficiently restored to swallow a cup of coffee, and though his hands were trembling so violently that he had cut himself while shaving, he looked presentable.

After breakfast I took him into the study, sat him in a

chair, stood over him and said to him . . . 'If this ever happens again I shall kill you.'

He began to rise from the chair, mumbling something about 'telling your mother', as he invariably did when he was thwarted. Then he remembered that she was not there to tell, to use as an instrument of blackmail, and he sank back, staring at me with a mixture of outrage and astonishment. Nobody had ever spoken to him like this before.

'I shall kill you,' I repeated. 'I want you to be quite clear about that. I shall kill you. How, I don't know. But I'm not a fool, and I shall find a way. Is that understood?'

Quite evidently, it was understood. The expression of outrage and astonishment was fading into one of genuine fear.

We drove home in silence. When I deposited him in the hall of the Haunted House my mother's pleasure and relief was very touching. So her plan had been a success! He had been alone for four days, had behaved himself, and had not touched a drop! And here he was again, looking so well! As she said this, searching his features for clues, I was happy that I had remembered to dab Max Factor on his chin, to conceal the tell-tale evidence of the razor-cuts.

And so to the first night, and the crowded audience, and the applause, and the supper at the Savoy – and the moment when I met my father's eyes, as he was about to lift a glass of champagne to drink my health. He set it down again, and drank to me in water.

There is a moral to this story. For six whole months he continued to abstain. I saw to that. I was constantly in and out of the Haunted House, and each time that we met, he got the message. It was not spoken; it was in my eyes; the intention, the desire, and the capacity – to kill. It may not have led to any demonstrations of paternal or filial affection, but at least it gave to all of us a respite of peace, and to my mother an illusion of happiness.

But it was only an interlude. At the end of this period I was called to America, and he began again.

174

Chapter Six ❧

Towards the middle of the thirties my mother began to die. Slowly, fitfully, over a period of three long years, in a series of crises that increased in gravity. The message was written on her face and in her eyes; she began to read it and to be frightened; and for that, again, she had to thank my father. *He* was arrogantly contemptuous of the thought of an after-life. There would be no rewards nor punishments, no heaven and – fortunately for himself – no hell. On the few occasions when his brain flickered back to the fires of his youth, he took great pleasure in denying her the consolations of religion. 'Don't kid yourself, old girl,' he used to say. 'You'll never pass through the Pearly Gates. There aren't any.' This was the ultimate in sadism. G. K. Chesterton once wrote that the greatest sin in the world was to break a child's toy. Like all paradoxes this is arguable, but it applied to my mother. Faith may be a spiritual toy, but in the curious playground of this world, it has served, to say the least of it, a useful purpose. To my mother it would have brought infinite consolation. But he broke the toy.

You could see the slow shadows of death gathering on her face. The shadows had no poetical tinge; they were red and ugly. Were this a novel, there would be a temptation to write that death advanced gracefully. But death has no habit of elegance, and in the last of life's wardrobes there are no disguises. Her cheeks did not pale. She began to develop a painful flush which caused her the greatest distress.

Sometimes she would stand in front of her bedroom mirror with her face in her hands, saying, 'I look terrible . . . my cheeks are burning so.' I would take away her hands and tell her that she was talking nonsense. But she was not. Here was this sinister flush, pulsing under the skin that had once rivalled the petals of a wild rose. I was blind not to realize that there was a deep-seated organic disturbance. Instead of consulting a doctor I used to go to Elizabeth Arden's for expensive creams and lotions, knowing only too well that she would never use them.

Meanwhile, at the outset of our pathetic little expeditions together to the cinema, to Hampton Court or Kew Gardens, I was obliged to listen, without protest, to my father's jocular comments about her appearance.

He would look up owlishly from his arm-chair, and stare at her, and say . . .

'Feeling the heat, m'dear?'

'Bit red about the gills . . . what?'

'Not been at the bottle, have you?'

Whereupon she would force a smile, and the one-time rose-petal cheeks would go redder still.

After these exchanges, when we went outside to hail a taxi, the procedure was always the same. A clutch at my arm, a sigh, the same sentence. 'You must remember that it is not *him*.'

Bitterly I reproach the succession of doctors who, when they had been called in to give sedatives to my father, had never noticed my mother's flaming cheeks, ignored her hurried breathing and trembling hands. It was not till she was within an ace of death that I took matters into my own hands.

It happened like this.

Paul rang me up from the vicarage in Cambridge Square. His voice was shaking.

'Mother is very ill indeed. Can you come round?'

'Of course.' And then, the inevitable question. 'How is He?'

'Just beginning.'

Paul rang off. He, the man of God, was certainly being put through his paces by his Master. As I drove through the noisy streets I thought of the raw deal that life had given him. Always *manqué*, always missing the boat. A brilliant preacher, but preaching to empty pews. A passionate nature, but with nobody to share it. A lover of youth and sunshine and laughter – growing old in a setting of darkness and despair, because he had taken up the cross of my father, and had sworn to bear it till the end.

Here let us allow ourselves another moment of comedy. In Grosvenor Square I stopped the car opposite Number 4, the home of Lady Cunard. I was dining with her that night; the Prime Minister would be there; and I wanted to jot down two amusing stories that I had heard the night before. Dining with Emerald was something of an ordeal; one never knew when she might rap the table and direct attention to oneself. Better be prepared. So I took out my pad, which was already scribbled over with numbers to ring up, people to interview, ideas for 'stories' and all the customary clutter of the journalistic trade. I jotted down the outline of the stories.

Then I turned the page and wrote this: '*Think re murder. Tabulate methods. Go British Museum. Babbacombe cliffs.*'

To the British Museum for book on poisons, to Babbacombe cliffs because they had dangerous escarpments. I had forgotten that these cliffs were on the outskirts of Torquay. My mind had reverted to my boyhood.

Then I drove on again. That it was a moment of comedy I can now appreciate, but it did not seem so funny at the time.

II

She could scarcely speak; she lay in bed with her cheeks flaming; she was very frightened and she did not make much sense. But she said one thing which gave a clue. She complained of double vision. Somewhere or other in my random reading of the past few days I had read that double vision was a sign of acute arterial tension.

'But, Mother, what is your blood pressure?'

'I don't know.'

'When did Doctor X last take it?'

'He has never taken it.'

I beckoned Paul outside.

'This is incredible. Is Doctor X mad?'

'I don't know what to think.'

'Why must we have Doctor X anyway?'

'*He* likes him.'

So there we were again. Back to my father, the *fons et origo* of all evil. *He* liked him. I had a shrewd suspicion that the reason he liked him was because Doctor X might be another drunk.

'We can't let Mother die. We've got to get a second opinion.'

'He'll be furious.'

'So what?'

Paul was very near to breaking point. 'He may come into her room and start shouting. I've tried so hard to keep him quiet. It's difficult.'

'It's total hell. Particularly for you. All the same we've got to get *somebody* . . . and quickly.'

'But who?'

Suddenly I knew the answer.

'Max.'

'But will he come? And what about medical etiquette?' Paul was leaning against the wall with his eyes closed. He was utterly exhausted and no longer capable of making a decision.

'Max is a relation and he could pretend to be making a friendly call. As for his coming, I'll see to that.'

I ran down the stairs, leaving Paul to guard the door.

Max Simpson, a distant cousin, was one of the few branches in the worthless tangle of our family tree who can be recalled without a shudder. It would have been too much to hope that he should have been 'normal'; nothing 'normal' ever sprang from that twisted trunk; he was homosexual and in my younger days had subjected me to furtive little dabs and prods, and suspiciously expensive presents. That sort of thing was easy to deal with, and after a time I grew quite fond of him, because he was the very epitome of 'normality' compared with the rest of the Nichols brood. I used to dine with him in his opulent flat off Grosvenor Square – (it was decorated in the period of Louis Seize and the Buhl tables were laden with his collection of snuff-boxes, some of which revealed 'naughtinesses' if you pressed the right button) – and while we were eating his delicious food I would look at him, and think . . . 'This is extraordinary. You are one of our family, however remotely related, and yet you are not a drunk, you are not a bully, you are not a miser and you are not, as far as one can observe, suffering from tertiary syphilis. You are just a plump, amusing, elegant old thing who dresses rather too well, eats rather too much, and uses rather too much scent in the bath and yet . . . you are one of us. How did this happen? Something must have gone wrong.'

Max was even socially 'sortable', indeed, he was a parody of a fashionable Mayfair physician. He worked in partnership with a man called Sir Bruce Bruce-Porter, who had such a mania for publicity that he nearly got into trouble with the British Medical Council. They had much in common; they both sported monocles, they both had grand motor-cars and a glittering clientele, and between them their bedside manners would have been enough to equip the entire diplomatic corps.

However, none of this seemed to matter, as I raced the car towards his consulting-room. Figure of fun he might be, but he was a brilliant doctor, with a special flair for diagnosis.

I caught him just as he was driving off to see the Grand Duchess Xenia. There was a brief, short struggle of wills. He would not keep the Grand Duchess waiting; it would be a gross breach of etiquette for him to intervene. I stood on the pavement repeating the same question. 'Did he want my mother to die?'

He came. An hour later my mother was being bled, as a desperate measure to reduce her blood pressure, which had risen to the menacing height of 240. In the hall, when he was taking his leave, Max said to me, 'Your mother is living with a bomb in her pocket.'

'Did you tell her?'

'Yes. It is essential that she should have no nervous strain.'

'Oh, Max!' Should one laugh or should one weep at such advice, in such a house, at such a moment?

Max shrugged his shoulders and took his leave.

I walked upstairs to see her. On the way I met Smith, a pleasant elderly housemaid who had managed to endure the turmoils of the vicarage for a whole year. She too looked as though she did not know whether to laugh or to weep.

'Is there anything the matter, Smith?'

'No, sir. It's only . . .' Then she decided to laugh. 'Mrs Nichols has just told me that my collar is not clean.' She shook her head. 'She's not always a very easy lady, sir.'

'Life has not always been very easy . . . for her.'

When I entered her room I saw, for a moment, a trace of the beauty that had once been hers. She had lost so much blood that the unhealthy flush had gone from her cheeks leaving them as pale as ivory. I took her hand; I did not want, just yet, to talk about her illness.

'What is this you have been saying to Smith?'

'Her collar was *not* clean.'

'I didn't notice it. You shouldn't notice so many things.'

'Somebody has to notice them.'

'Not for a while. The end of the world won't come if there's a little dust on the drawing-room mantelpiece.'

She managed a smile. That was better. I bent down, gave her a kiss, and left her to sleep.

·   ·   ·   ·   ·

The end, as I have indicated, was drawing near, and as I recall its gradual approach I am filled with regret that the picture of my mother in these pages should have been so shadowy. True, she lived in the shadows, but she was a figure of light, and the light should have shone through the story, and illuminated these pages. It has not done so. No doubt this is partly due to my own short-comings as a biographer. In a work of fiction it would have been easy to make her convincing, for in moments of dramatic crisis the author of fiction can give his heroine an added stature; at his command are all the familiar devices of the flashing eye, the defiant toss of the head, the whitening cheeks, the ringing challenge of the voice. My mother's life was an unending complex of crises, but she did not react in so physically appealing a manner. Her eyes did not flash, they blinked; her cheeks did not whiten, they flushed most painfully; her voice did not rise, it sank to a whisper, and there were times when what she whispered was nonsense. I have often wondered what went on in her brain, as opposed to what went on in her heart and her spirit. What sort of brain *was* it? Such a question, surely, is neither unkind nor unintelligent; any man is entitled to speculate on the nature of his genes. 'Why,' he can ask himself, 'did I turn this way and not the other? By what frail spiders' thread of inherited instincts was I guided? How direct was the tug of the umbilical cord? Where was it knotted; and where did it break off altogether?'

Very amateur psychological inquiries, no doubt, but worth the asking. Why was my mother entranced by Chaminade and bored by Mozart? Why did she live so vividly in the pages of *Wuthering Heights* while she could not read a word of Emily Brontë's poetry? Why was she so totally devoid of 'taste?' Why the dark-brown wall-papers, the distressing 'ornaments', the bogus pictures, all indicating an apparently total inability to distinguish between what was beautiful – for she had inherited a few beautiful things – and what was atrocious?

Consider the various mantelpieces in these drawing-rooms. They never changed. Whatever the nature of the house we were living in, large or small, light or dark, ancient or modern, the drawing-room mantelpiece was sacrosanct. It supported a bewildering clutter of objects for which there was not even any sentimental justification. Occasionally, when she was out, I would remove some of the rubbish that had accumulated over the years – the Irish china pigs, the faded photographs, the nouveau art vases, the horse-brasses, the Indian sandalwood boxes, the enamel coffee-spoons, the Japanese 'curios' and such-like. But when my mother saw what had been done, she was greatly upset. Not a thing must be altered. As it was in the beginning, so it must remain, from this time forth for evermore. It was an aesthetic interpretation of the marriage service.

I was constantly assured, by both my mother and my father, that these things were 'good' (which meant expensive) and because they were 'good' they must therefore be beautiful. The dining-room furniture was heavy and cumbersome, dominated by a 'suite' of dark Edwardian Gothic, and I used to wonder why I hated it so much. But there were worse horrors. Most dreadful of all was a standard lampshade, standing on a cluster of brass claws, supporting a bloated centre-piece of bright orange glass. This literally frightened me; it was like a foetus which I had once seen bottled in a museum. After this, the most odious of our possessions was an enormous china model of a Negress clutching a pannier of painted fruit. It has been a wedding present from a woman of title, and therefore, of course was 'good', and must be beautiful.

The Negress reminds me of the dancing faun, and this recollection may perhaps bring my mother into clearer focus.

The dancing faun was a reproduction of the celebrated creation of Brancusi. It was about three feet high, wrought in a metal which had acquired pleasing patina, and it was almost the only thing to which, today, I would give house room. But in the eyes of my mother, the faun had a fatal defect. He had lost his fig-leaf. Admittedly, the physical revelations of this misadventure could not be described as startling; the organ, so unfortunately exposed, was almost invisible. But, with the aid of a magnifying glass, a pair of prying eyes could detect the faun's unquestionable masculinity.

So what was to be done?

What my mother did was totally idiotic, and symbolic of the whole tragi-comedy of our existence. Again and again, over the years, in spring and summer and winter, she expended her energies in collecting bunches of flowers to set at the feet of the faun in order to conceal his diminutive potentials. The faun was 'good', so the faun must stand, as he always stood, on the main staircase, whether the staircase was wide and sweeping, as at Cleave Court, or steep and narrow, as in some of our other houses. But the proprieties must be observed, and these proprieties necessitated a thick shield of antirrhinums in summer, disposed around the hips, or –when flowers were scarce – a potted fern or a bunch of bracken.

The faun, and her reaction to his nakedness, symbolized the grotesque contrasts of her life. As a girl she had been gently nurtured. Her youth was spent in a large and quite pretty house in Yorkshire, and though her family had not been distinguished, there had been kindness and there had been money. Quite a lot of money. (One of my father's favourite stories – told with great bonhomie at our tea-parties – involved a quotation from his own grandfather, who had reminded him, when he was seeking my mother's hand, that 'though there may be a lot of pretty girls without money there are also a lot of pretty girls *with* money'. After which he would leer at my mother, commanding her to smile, which of course she did.) Some of this money was expended on her education. She was sent to a convent in Passy, a suburb on the outskirts of Paris, where the girls were sternly disciplined, and where any sort of masculine contacts were taboo. I remember her telling me how she had once been walking down a corridor when one of the sisters had run towards her and pushed her into a dark cupboard, lest she should encounter the laundry-man, who was on his way up the stairs. On returning from Paris, she fell into the normal routine of a Victorian young lady, which, in the wilds of Yorkshire, was even more strictly conventional than it would have been in London.

And that reminds me of a story.

III

One evening I called at the Haunted House in Cambridge Square on my way to the theatre. I was in white tie and tails and my mother asked if I was going to a party.

'No,' I said. 'It's the first night of *The Importance of Being Earnest.*'

Her face fell. 'Oscar Wilde's play?'

'Of course.'

'Oh dear. I suppose I'm old-fashioned. But how can you go to a play by such a person?'

I began to reply that it happened to be a very good play, but she was not listening.

'If I had guessed about Wilde when he was staying with us in Yorkshire . . .' she began.

It was my turn to interrupt. 'When Wilde was *what*?'

'He was lecturing in Leeds,' she explained, 'and your grandmother invited him. Everybody who came to Leeds used to stay with us.'

'But why didn't you tell me this before?'

In complete seriousness she replied: 'I did not think that it was the sort of thing that one cared to mention.'

I recall this episode in order to illustrate the almost unbelievable time-lapse between my mother's present and her past – or rather, the *lack* of a time-lapse, for her whole men-
184

tality was geared to the nineties, and it was my father who made sure that it stayed there.

At length, with many hesitations and excuses and shakings of the head, she told me about Wilde's visit, ending with an enchanting breakfast scene, when – spurning the elaborate collection of dishes on my grandmother's sideboard – he had plaintively inquired if he might perhaps have a few raspberries – pale *yellow* raspberries. A request which, in snow-bound Yorkshire, a week before Christmas, she was unable to satisfy. However, I have told this story before, and since it has been reprinted in a number of Wilde anthologies, my only excuse for mentioning it again is to emphasize the fact that my mother, at my father's behest, was constricted, twisted, perverted – choose what word you will – into a parody of the gentle, tolerant woman that she might have been.

Chapter Seven ❧

She died on June 20th, 1939. This is the longest day of the year; and for those who waited on her passing it was the longest day of their lives.

Time and again, in the years that have intervened, I have tried to set on paper the emotions of that day – gone to an empty room, taken up a pen, begun to write. But this is a fragment of autobiography that will not be written; the words falter, the pen is laid aside. It is like what happened on the following day, when she lay cold and alone in the Haunted House. I had an engagement to make a speech at – of all things – the opening of a roof garden in a London store. The event had been widely publicized, there would be a crowd of celebrities, and a film company was to make a news-reel of the occasion. My impulse, when, late at night, I recollected the engagement, was to get somebody to telephone and say that I couldn't come. Then, I thought better of it. She would have wanted me to go, so I went, took my place on the platform, looked out on to banks of potted plants and stretches of new-laid turf, and heard the sound of fountains and tinkling streams, against the distant throb of traffic below. Then my name was called and I rose to speak. I had prepared nothing to say, which was just as well, because I could not speak at all. The fountains went on playing and the streams still tinkled, but the cameras stopped turning, and that is all I remember. A long time afterwards a woman who was sitting on the platform told me that I had, in fact, spoken five words. 'You said ". . . she was a great gardener".' To whom was I referring? I told her that I had no idea. She nodded in sympathy. 'We all realized that you were obviously unwell.'

186

My mother's face, in death, was a tortured mask. The fact that it was so twisted, so agonized, came with all the greater shock because this was the first time that I had ever looked on the face of the dead.

I went into the room where they had taken her when the end was near. There was a sickly scent of lilies; the windows were open and the curtains were stirring in the summer breeze. When I shut the door they fell back into place and there was total silence and stillness.

Then I stepped over to the bed, and for a moment all the other emotions were swept away by a sense of outraged surprise. Throughout my life I had been comforted by the illusion that with death there comes a respite to the body, and that this release is mirrored in the features, as though gentle fingers had smoothed away the lines of pain. I had even heard, and had believed, that in some cases there was a strange radiance, as though, in dying, there had been a sudden glimpse of paradise.

But it was all a lie. Whatever else one might read into that mask there was no message of peace or comfort. It was the face of a woman on the rack, and this was made all the more appalling by the fact that one knew that the torture, so clearly reflected, could have had no physical cause. She had been in no great pain, and, in any case, she had been for days under heavy sedation. What one was seeing was a soul in torment.

Then the door opened, and my father appeared. So powerful was his presence, so dark and dominating, that for a moment the figure on the bed was forgotten. But there was something else about him that gave an extra twist to the screws of fear – something new, and quite inexplicable. As soon as he had entered, the instant built-in computer reactions of my brain had begun the familiar questionings. Which stage of drunkenness had he reached? Was he at the beginning – in the middle – nearing the end? It was important to have a correct answer to these questions; in a few days my mother would be laid to rest, there would be all the gruesome paraphernalia of the funeral, the gathering of relations, the disposal of her worldly goods. For her sake, if for no other reason, it was vital that he should be reasonably presentable, that he should 'pull himself together'.

But as he stepped into the light I suddenly realized that these fears were groundless. My mental computer was giving no answer to the routine questions which normally would have been solved in the space of a few seconds. He was neither drunk, nor recovering from drink, nor beginning to drink. He had suddenly acquired a strange and almost arrogant sobriety which, paradoxically, made him all the more menacing than before.

I was soon to learn the explanation, and when we come to it we shall reach the bitter core of our story.

Meanwhile, through all the pain and misery of these days, I had one unfailing source of comfort . . . sordid, material, and, you may say, even despicable. It was a typed document of three pages, signed with my mother's name.

II

A few weeks before her death, my mother made her only gesture of independence in forty years of married life. She drew up a new will, leaving her modest estate to be divided between my brothers and myself. When she signed it she was sitting in bed, propped up on the pillows with an old shawl round her shoulders, and an expression of bewilderment and fear. By her side was Paul, trying to explain its meaning to her. But it was a long time before she could bring herself to write her name. Her eyes kept straying towards the ceiling. Supposing *he* were to come down? Paul reminded her that it would be at least two days before he would be able to get out of bed. But supposing he were to find out, when he was better? 'He will never find out,' said Paul, 'unless you tell him.' 'But I have never kept anything from him,' she said, 'not till now; I have had no secrets, told him no lies.' In an agony of impatience, for I too had this unreasoning fear that he might come down, I muttered, 'More's the pity' – and instantly regretted it, because of the look of pain that it brought to her face.

At last she signed, screwing up her eyes as though she did not wish to see what her fingers were doing.

What was the occasion of this family conference? And what prompted her to take a step so alien to her nature?

I must take some of the responsibility. Although my father had always been secretive about his financial standing, I had a rough idea of the condition of his fortunes. It was not healthy. He had no real estate. (The house in Cambridge Square was the perquisite of Paul, who was entitled to live in it only so long as he remained vicar of St Michael's.) If the contents had been put for sale, they might have fetched five hundred pounds. My father's securities had a value of approximately three thousand pounds, and they were not the sort of securities that a sensible man would have cared to own.

But he still had one asset – a portfolio of solid industrials, with a market value of ten thousand pounds, which was all that remained of my mother's marriage settlement. During her life-time he could not touch this capital, but it would be his, all his, on the day she died. He had caused her to draw up a will leaving him all her assets, to dispose of as he wished with no mention of my brothers or myself.

I cannot remember how we discovered the existence of this document, but when it fell into my hands I felt a natural indignation. Not on my own account, for by our family's standards I was quite rich. But Alan had almost nothing, and Paul had to subsist on his parson's pittance.

When he got his hands on this money, what would he do with it? There were several answers to that question, all distasteful. My own conviction, later to be confirmed, was that he would get another woman, probably a barmaid. He

189

was still 'a fine figure of a man'. In his late seventies, admittedly, but still 'six foot in his socks' (when he was able to stand upright), and, of course, a 'gentleman'. Oh, yes – John Nichols Esquire, with £10,000 worth of gilt-edged securities in his pocket, might spend several more pleasurable years in poisoning the earth.

This must not happen, at all costs it must be prevented. This was not easy to contrive, for Paul had all my mother's gentleness, reluctance, and hesitancy. But at length the will was drawn up and, as we have seen, she signed it.

This piece of paper became for me the most precious document in the world. Not for any material advantage but as an instrument of revenge.

Chapter Eight ✍

Four days passed, or was it five? Not that it matters, for here is another of those pieces of autobiography that refuse to be written. The funeral, in the churchyard of Long Ashton, near Bristol – the preparatory hotel luncheon, the pale sheep-like masks of the mourners – the rain beating on the tattered wreaths. I am still not able to consider these things dispassionately.

But I can still *report*, clearly, accurately, and with a cleansing sense of hatred at long last attaining its objective.

We are in the car, my father and I, speeding on our way to the South Coast. The funeral is over; the last mourners have departed. And here am I with her murderer – for how else can he be described? – on our way to – of all places – the bustling sea-port of Plymouth.

How did this grotesque situation come about? The explanation is simple. When she was dead I took, as it were, a deep breath, and said to myself, 'I will make one last effort to forgive, to forget, to try to see, even for a few hours, what *she* had seen in this man whom once she had loved.'

So I went to him and said, 'When the funeral is over, you may be feeling too upset to go back to Cambridge Square. Besides, it might be better if Paul were to have a few days to himself. Would you care to come away with me for a few days?'

Not unnaturally, he was surprised by this suggestion. He was under no illusions about the way I felt towards him, and for a moment he hesitated, staring at me suspiciously, as though he wondered whether I were planning another attempt on his life.

'Where were you thinking of going?'

'Wherever you choose. We'd have the car. And stay at a comfortable hotel. You'd be my guest.'

He continued to stare at me. And then – because he must have realized that I was actually sincere in my desire to help – he broke into a smile. 'That's very kind of you, m'boy,' he muttered. 'Very kind indeed.' He cleared his throat and I feared that he might be going into his familiar act about 'your poor old father – no good to anybody – can't think why you put up with me'. I was spared the variations on this familiar theme. Instead, screwing up his monocle and bracing his shoulders, he said, 'What about Plymouth?'

'Plymouth?' It was my turn to stare. Of all places in the world, why Plymouth? I had, and have, nothing against this prosperous sea-port, but on the only occasion that I had visited it, it had seemed brash and noisy and restless. One might as well go to Manchester or Birmingham. For that matter, one might as well stay in London. Why Plymouth?

Then he gave the explanation. His smile broadened. 'Lots of pretty girls in Plymouth,' he said.

I nodded. So be it. In the space of a few seconds, with a single slash of cruelty, most skilfully delivered, he had killed my pathetic effort at reconciliation.

'Splendid,' I said. 'I'll book us at the Queen's Hotel.'

'Isn't that a bit expensive?'

'I can afford it.'

We smiled at each other, and I went off to telephone, to make the reservations.

Yes, I could afford it. The document in my pocket took care of that. My mother's will, of which he had no knowledge or suspicion. Well, he would know soon enough. The revelation had to be made to him, and since it would be a most ugly revelation, bitter and ruthless and uncompromising, calculated to hurt, it was better that it should be delivered on an ugly stage.

Yes, Plymouth was the ideal place. As I lifted the receiver it occurred to me that my father, in choosing this locale, may have had the makings of a dramatist.

Before we had been travelling for ten minutes, my father had made a remarkable recovery. His bowler hat was perched jauntily on the back of his head, the monocle was screwed in at a rakish angle, and the voice no longer faltered. He suggested a man who had been lunching at a City banquet rather than one who had just attended the funeral of his wife.

He became talkative. At first I did not pay much attention to what he was saying, for I had heard it all before. As though from a far distance I recognized the familiar word 'syphilis', as applied to my Aunt Blanche, who had attended the funeral with some reluctance, because it had involved her in an expenditure of nearly two pounds, what with the taxi fare and the cost of the wreath. How pale she had looked, how obviously diseased, and how curious it was that her flesh had not yet rotted on her bones! And my Uncle George – obviously he had syphilis too. It was 'written all over him'. Well, their day would come, and he for one would not be sorry to see it. He might not have made much of a success out of his life, but at least he had kept himself clean.

With such topics did my father beguile me as we drove along. Then he suddenly changed the subject. Through the drone of his conversation came the word 'Alhambra'. I knew what that meant – women, the women of his youth. And I knew why he was recalling them at this, of all moments. It was to give an extra twist to the knife, to rub a final pinch of salt into the wound. The cruelty of it was so outrageous, even from him, that as my hands tightened on the steering wheel, I had a momentary impulse to crash the car into the ditch. Then I remembered the will, and reflected that it was better for him to live and to suffer, and I prayed that he might live long, and suffer to the utmost. So I stared straight ahead and listened, while my father– with many side-glances in my direction to see how his stories were affecting me – evoked the prostitutes of long ago.

He had a vivid turn of phrase, and as he warmed to his task, the women of the Alhambra came clearly into view, blotting out the fading figure of my mother. I saw them parading through the lush corridors of the old music-hall, preening themselves in the gilded mirrors, flaunting their feathered hats. In the background, twirling a cane and twisting his moustache, I saw the figure of my father – young, handsome, lusty, with the seed of my own life in his loins. I wondered how much of that seed had entered the bodies of the women he had pleasured, and if any of it had borne fruit. I had no need to wonder what type of women they were, for he was only too anxious to bring them clearly before me. They were all of a pattern, dark and heavy-breasted. Their breasts, in particular, in shape, in colour, and in response. So eloquent did he wax that I could almost smell their bodies, mingling with the fresh country air that drifted through the windows.

A spasm of revulsion twitched my hand, and for a moment the car headed for a tree. I swung it back on to the road, but the shock was enough to make my father sit up abruptly, and bring his recitation to a close. 'Keep your eye on the ball, old chap,' he muttered. He took up his monocle and wiped it. 'Don't want to go before my time.'

II

The Queen's Hotel was hardly the place that I should have chosen as a setting for my grief. Had I been my own master, I should have gone off to the Yorkshire moors, to Haworth, because this was the place to which I had taken my mother on our last journey together and because it was the last time in our lives when we had been alone. I should have liked to wander through the parsonage, to sit in the churchyard, and look out on to the lonely moorland. In that wild countryside I might have seen her shadow on the heather, caught her voice in the wind.

Instead, I had to listen to my father's dramatic sniffs as he signed the register. A press photographer had been waiting on the steps, much to his satisfaction, and as soon as he saw him, he resumed his role of a bereaved husband and the fond father of a celebrated author. The manager was all solicitude. My father was such a charming old gentleman –so distinguished, so obviously stricken. They would do everything in their power to assuage his grief. Yes, I said, that would be very kind of them. And would he like a sitting-room to himself? Yes. By all means. And I managed to smile at him as he went up in the lift.

That night I went mad; for I was very near to breaking point. As I went from pub to pub, incongruously attired in black, I found myself coming back to life. Life on the off-beat, life at its crudest, life like a gulp of neat whisky – but at least life. I found my fingers flicking to the music of the cracked pianos. I began to remember the words of the dirty songs the sailors were singing. The dirtier the better. At the bar my arms stretched out for the friendly shoulders of the matelots who were taking my money. That night I was rich; that night I was gay; that night I was plunged in the pit of the ultimate despair. But even in the last degradation, when I woke up in a strange bedroom, in a boarding-house by the docks, I knew that my mother would have understood. I looked up at the dirty ceiling and smiled. It was a smile without a trace of shame – a smile that said 'Now, at last, you understand.'

Dawn was breaking when I returned to the Queen's Hotel. I had passed a rough night, in every sense of the word, my garments of mourning were stained and crumpled, my pockets were empty, and I had a nasty bruise on my forehead, but I felt purified and at peace. I walked out to the public gardens and stared at the asphalt sea. It was peopled with the dim shapes of ships lying at anchor, like animals that have not yet been awakened. In a few weeks those ships would be at war.

Chapter Nine ✦

Saturday dawned dank and cheerless with a grey mist coming in from the sea. This must be the day of reckoning, the day on which the existence of the will would be disclosed. There was no time to lose, because we had already passed – or so I assumed – the period in which he would begin again. At the moment he was still taking only water, which he ordered loudly and ostentatiously at the dining-table, while I sipped my glass of wine. This could not go on for long. By the following afternoon, at the latest, he would have started on his first pint of strong ale, which would lead swiftly and ineluctably to the first bottle of whisky, and so on, to the bitter end of the pattern.

It was essential, when the revelation was made, that he should be sober. There must be no softening of the shock; it must be stunning and absolute.

I spent the morning laying plans for the *scène à faire*. Where should it be, in public or in private? At first I was inclined to think that it would be best played in his suite. There were a hundred things to be said – a life-time of things – and I could not hear myself saying them in public. Some of them would have to be clothed in very crude words – the words he had taught me since I was a child. Then I wondered. Might it not be better to play it cool? This would be one of the great moments in my life and it must not degenerate into a shouting match; it must be composed as the bitterest of comedies. This demanded an audience. So I decided on the sun-parlour of the hotel lounge, setting the action in the far corner, where there was a comfortable chair reserved for important guests. Since our arrival, my father had occupied it.

There were a number of theatrical advantages for this setting. He would have his face to the light and I would have the pleasure of seeing that face puffed and poisoned by the hatred that he would be feeling for me. Again, the chair was so designed that it would be difficult to get out of in a hurry. I wanted no sudden exits; he must hear me to the end. But perhaps the most compelling reason for choosing this part of the hotel was the fact that we should be within earshot of the after-luncheon crowd at the neighbouring tables. He had made friends among them. They were the sort of people he liked, and he had made free with my name in order to ingratiate himself. It was the same technique that he had employed ever since I became a 'celebrity'. 'Yes,' he would say, 'Beverley is my son. Wouldn't think it, would you? Not much brains myself.' (Pause for contradiction.) 'But then, I never had his chances. Never went to a public school. Never went to Oxford.' (Pause for a long sigh.) '*He* had the best of everything. Mind you, it was a sacrifice, but I don't regret it. Not a penny of it.'

II

We lunched early, and now – assured that there were several hours of sobriety before us – I suggested that he might like to have a glass of sherry. To my surprise, he declined. No, he replied, he would not care for any sherry. 'But don't let me stop you, my boy'.

I felt a twinge of apprehension. Something strange was happening. The real-life drama had taken an unexpected twist; the star was acting out of character. True, the stage directions had required him to be sober, but not so unnaturally sober as this. A small glass of sherry would set the infernal chemistry of his body on the familiar path to destruction; it would have given a warm glow which would have made all the more sharp the impending chill of disillusionment. But the thirst seemed to have gone out of him completely. His eyes were clear; his hand was steady, I might have been sitting opposite a stranger.

He began to talk about his future plans. At last, the drama began to play itself as I had intended. Perhaps, he said, he might buy a cottage somewhere in this part of the world. Yes, I agreed, that might be a very good idea.

'When everything's settled,' he went on, 'and when your poor mother's affairs are wound up, I'll be able to rub along, quite nicely. After all, there's a lot one can do with ten thousand pounds.'

As he spoke, he leant forward slightly, studying my reaction to this remark, which was intended to shock. For all he knew, I was unaware of the amount of my mother's estate, nor how she had disposed of it.

I did not react. I let him continue with his little day-dream.

Then came the familiar twisting of the knife. At his time of life, he continued, it might not be a bad idea to invest the whole sum in an annuity. He could get a safe tax-free 12 per cent. What did I think of that? Again he leant forward to study my reaction. Had it not been for the document in my pocket, I might have told him what I thought of it. But I was able to answer his suggestions with a smile. An annuity? Yes, he should certainly buy an annuity. At which a fleeting look of suspicion passed over his face. The conversation was not going as he had intended; the knife was not twisting home. Here he was, with all this money at his disposal, threatening to withdraw it irrevocably from the reach of myself and my brothers, and I was betraying no emotion whatsoever.

Suddenly he said: 'I think I'll have a glass of wine after all.'

'Of course.' This was just as I would have wished. Just one glass. But it must be the last before the denouement.

He gulped it greedily, wiped his moustache with his napkin, sighed, and relaxed.

Now came the final twist of the knife – now, perhaps more

than at any other time in his life, he revealed himself as the naked sadist that he was. The wine worked instantly, waking the devil inside him, impelling him to hurt me. He set down his glass, looked me straight in the eyes and said: 'Yes – the prospect's pretty rosy. I might get another woman.'

'Yes, you might.'

We stared at one another, both smiling in our separate ways – hatred meeting hatred.

'Nothing to do with marriage,' said my father. 'I've had enough of that.' He made an obscene gesture with his hands, in the curve of a woman's breast. 'Just an obliging little body, with plenty of the upper story.'

This was my cue. My hand began to travel towards my breast pocket, but it travelled slowly. For though the scene was set as a comedy, the veils of tragedy were enveloping it. And this, surely, was the acrid essence of tragedy even if it was played in a vulgar setting, and even if the heart of the matter was centred in ten thousand pounds of gilt-edged securities.

I had had just about enough.

'Coffee?'

'I could do with a cup.'

I helped him out of the chair. It was repulsive even to feel the touch of his body through his heavy suit. But the drama must go on – we must go to our appointed places.

I sat him in his corner. The waiter brought the coffee. The phantoms of the mists outside were darkening and grouping themselves like figures in a Greek tragedy.

I remained standing over him. The theatrical positions were precisely as I had foreseen. The bloated body in the chair, the light on his face, and the required amount of publicity.

'I think I'll go out for a short walk,' I said. 'Just for twenty minutes or so. Will you be here when I get back? Good. Because there's something I think you ought to read.'

I drew out the will. It was enclosed in a thick linen envelope and the lawyer's clerk had addressed it to 'John Nichols Esquire', in copperplate script.

He stared at the envelope. 'What is it?'

'You'll see.'

III

If I ever go to Plymouth again, I shall always see it as it was on that desolate afternoon, as I walked up and down the Hoe, staring out to sea, where the ships were lying in the shadow of approaching war. Normally, as an adult and reasonably thoughtful citizen, my thoughts would have been concerned with that war, and the part I might or might not play in it. But now the scene was overshadowed by a black, obese figure slumped in an arm-chair behind the window of the Queen's Hotel, a hundred yards away.

Twenty minutes pass. Maybe they should have been twenty minutes of mounting anger – maybe I should have polished my farewell speech, checked on my final entrance. It was not at all like that. As I walked back to the hotel all I felt was a sense of almost unbearable fatigue.

For this reason, I will ring down the curtain quickly, summing it up in three lines.

Two of them were spoken by my father, as he greeted me on my return. He was still in the chair where I had left him, staring straight ahead. His face was purple and the veins were swelling out of his forehead. When our eyes met he gasped . . .

'Is this bloody thing a fake?'

I told him no. It was quite in order.

Then he said . . . 'In that case I've only got £3,000 in the world, to last for the rest of my life.'

This pleased me; it conjured up visions of an old age of poverty and hardship. But I still felt none of the exultation which I had anticipated.

The final line was spoken by myself. Before I write it, I must explain why it is so important.

In all the years that had gone before, wherever he had given a particularly outrageous performance in the Haunted Houses of the past, and whenever I, or Paul or Alan, had tried to intervene, to bring him to his senses, he had invariably tottered to his feet, shuffled to the door, turned to us and said . . . 'I'll tell your mother.'

Again and again . . . 'I'll tell your mother.' Then he had paused, at the door, with his fingers on the handle, sneering at us, gloating in the potential of his blackmail. For we knew, all too well, what would be involved. He would stagger upstairs and tell her that we were going to 'knock him about'. He would clutch his heart and protest that he was in pain. He would call on her pity. This would throw her into acute distress, even though she knew that he was lying. So we would unclench our fists, sick at heart, and let him go.

My final line was prompted by a physical gesture on his part. He shuffled forward in the chair, beginning to drag himself up by the arms. As he did so his eyes searched the ceiling. He was looking 'upstairs', towards the figure to whom he had always called, in his hours of travail. He was about to say it again. 'I'll tell your mother.'

Then I bent down and picked up the will.

'There's nobody there,' I said. 'Nobody upstairs. Nobody left for you to hurt. Nobody to blackmail, any more.'

IV

And now we come to the strangest passage of this unhappy tale – and, in its implication, the most appalling.

My father never drank again.

To the student of alcoholism this must sound incredible. Here was a man who for over forty years had lived in order to drink, and drank in order to live. He had drunk enough to send a dozen men to an early grave. The whole pattern of his life, and of the lives of his family was dominated by alcohol. Month after month, year after year, he had subjected his body and his brain to an incessant ordeal of violent stimuli. He had literally *fed* on alcohol, denying himself almost any other form of nutriment for weeks on end. One would have thought that his liver must be rotted beyond repair and that his brain would be damaged beyond redemption. It would never have occurred to the most sanguine optimist that at this stage of his life he could have changed his ways. And yet that is precisely what happened. Although he was destined to live for eight more years, the glass of wine that he had taken at our valedictory luncheon was the last he was to drink before his death.

As I said above, to the student of alcoholism this must sound incredible, and those with whom I have discussed the matter – the Harley Street specialists – the pioneers of the brave band of Alcoholics Anonymous – the hypnotists and the faith healers – have all agreed that my father's case-history is unique in their experience. Such things, they protest, simply do not happen. Even if he made an heroic struggle, sought psychological assistance, taken courses of the most drastic drugs, his sudden abandonment of alcohol would have been little less than a miracle.

But he did none of these things, he made no struggle, sought no assistance, took no drugs. He simply stopped.

If that is indeed so, reply the experts, we have no explanation.

But I have an explanation, and I have already given it in an earlier passage of this book. My father was possessed. If this is a psychic diagnosis, it is none the worse for that, for those – at any rate – who happen like myself to believe in the devil. And even if it *is* a psychic diagnosis it is the only one that accords with the otherwise totally inexplicable medical history. My father surrendered himself to the devil, and having done so, selected my mother as the principal victim of the sadism that had been implanted in him.

And when the victim was removed by death, he laid down his glass.

Chapter Ten ✤

Here, maybe, this book should end, and no doubt many people will suggest that it ought never to have been written at all. But there are still some loose ends to tie up.

After his departure from Plymouth my father went back to the Haunted House, and my brother Paul gave him shelter for the rest of his life. This was an act of simple Christian charity that would have been beyond me. To have known that he was sleeping under the same roof, to have been obliged to see him at every meal, even though his eyes were now bright and his complexion, unbelievably, as clear and clean as a young man's – I could not have endured it.

But then Paul – he would ask for no higher compliment – was nearer to my mother, in character and in temperament than I had ever been. I am not suggesting that he was a natural instrument for the attentions of a sadist. In her case, this was certainly true. If all the Powers that be had employed their Higher Intelligences over thousands of years, in order to create two people who were so surely doomed to destroy one another, they could not have succeeded with more exquisite precision than when they brought my parents together. Not so with Paul. He had a manly independence and he shared my detestation of cruelty in any form. But he had a strain of humility which enabled him to accept situations that I could not accept. Besides, he was the eldest; he had, as it were, to do the pioneer work in our distracted efforts to form some sort of pattern out of our broken lives.

Again, Paul had not the temperament of the artist. I had, and because I interpreted life in terms of the artist my father was a hideous discord in melodies that I might have composed, a gross blot on canvas that I might have painted, an intolerable interruption in stories that I might have told. Paul would never have tried to murder him. It was inevitable that I should do so for the simple reason that he was murdering me. It was a matter of self-defence, the eternal obligation of the artist to express himself and to destroy anything that might thwart this obligation.

Paul never felt the intensity of this hatred, because he had not the same reason for feeling it. God knows, he had causes enough, of one sort or another, but he was not so constantly tortured by the sense of talents thwarted and powers unfulfilled. Besides, he lacked the quality of ruthlessness which compelled me to examine my father under the microscope and to see him as he really was. Maybe this is only to say that Paul was a better Christian than myself, and that he had, and still has, the power to see good in all God's creatures.

Was there no good in my father? No good at all? Paul would say that there was. The true Christian, I suppose, must always say that. Yes. But where was this 'good'? Where, and when, and in what manner, was it ever evinced? The conventional Christian answer, presumably, is that there must have been good, because, like all men, he was a 'son of God'. But what *is* a 'son of God'? To me, the phrase is musty and meaningless, it has the sort of odour that comes from the pages of an ancient prayer book, secreted in one of the cupboards of a haunted house, whose pages are stained with whisky.

But that is not answering the question. Perhaps I can help to answer it by stressing one aspect of this father of mine which may indeed be unique. *He had no friends*. This statement is to be taken quite literally. He had no friends whatsoever, young or old, male or female, rich or poor. Nobody ever wrote to him, nobody ever rang him up, nobody ever sent him a Christmas card, nobody ever called to pass the time of day. It was as though he lived in a vacuum, in which friendship could play no part, a cold empty place where none wished – or dared – to join him.

Was this not strange? How had it happened, and why? There was something utterly unnatural in this bleak aloneness. Even the humblest old age pensioner has some friend with whom he can have a Christmas cup of tea. Even the most arrogant tycoon has some friend – it might only be a 'little woman round the corner' – who will sigh for him on occasions, though it may be only because the monthly cheque has not arrived. But my father had nobody. Why? He was not rich, but neither was he penniless. He had a façade of *bonhomie*. He had a sweet and gentle wife, three sons who were not unattractive in their various ways, and a succession of shabby but fairly elegant houses. And yet no friends ever crossed the thresholds of these houses. Indoors, in his own domain, he loomed like a gigantic, all-shadowing ghost, dominating all our lives, creeping down every corridor, darkening every window. But when he stepped out of the circle of his power he was alone, and when he returned to it, nobody followed him. Not even a stray dog.

Was this not strange? Was it not almost uncanny? Can it be explained by any other theory than the aura of evil with which I have invested him – an aura which was felt instinctively by those who had the misfortune to cross his path?

Here is a small but significant episode which may reinforce my theory. In the Plymouth *scène à faire*, after he had recovered from the initial shock which my revelation had given him, he showed himself completely impervious to all that had been said. He sat in his chair like a wounded animal, filled with a dark resentment because its fangs had been withdrawn, listening with total indifference to my Speech for the Prosecution – a speech which I had been rehearsing for twenty years. I accused him of every crime in the calendar and he merely yawned. Towards the end I told him that

I prayed for the existence of a literal hell, in which he might burn for ever. His answer was a sneering smile. Then, in a final fling I said to him – 'Do you realize that you haven't a friend in the world? Not one? Quite a number of people have often prayed that you would die, there is not one who would wish you to live. Not one. Why?'

The reaction was instant; the cut went home to the bone; it was as though I had suddenly pierced his armour.

From under his moustache a word came mumbling. I did not understand. 'What did you say?'

'Everidge.'

'What does that mean? Is it somebody's name?'

He did not reply. But the pronouncement of the word seemed to have given him a sudden reassurance. He hoisted himself out of his chair, and went up to his room to pack.

Some ten days later, after returning to London, I received a letter with a Bristol postmark. It was in a long, faded envelope, that looked as though it had lain for years in a lawyer's office. It was signed . . . 'Respectfully yours, J. D. Everidge'. Yes, said the writer, he certainly remembered Mr John Nichols, whom he had served as solicitor's clerk at the turn of the century. A very talented gentleman with a great future before him. He had often wondered what had happened to him. There followed a passage about the hardness of life and the pains of arthritis. The letter ended with a delicate hint that perhaps, for old times' sake, I might care to come to his assistance.

I wrote him out a cheque and sent it to my father, suggesting that he might care to send it to his 'friend'. I have often wondered if Everidge was another drunk.

II

My father died on a winter's night, in the last Haunted House – my brother Paul's vicarage at Southport in Lancashire. Paul kept his trust to the end, doing as my mother would have wished him to do, taking upon his overburdened shoulders the vows which she had taken in the marriage service. A life that many would say was utterly wasted. I do not think so; nor, I hope, does he.

Like the ageing star of an outmoded melodrama, making a 'positively final appearance' in the provinces, my father passed away in the same stage-setting, surrounded by all the ancient props and trappings of our other Haunted Houses, which Paul had faithfully transported with him. The vicarage at Southport was modest compared with the spurious grandeurs of Cleave Court and Cambridge Square, but the bogus family portraits still stared down from the walls, the heavy black Victorian Gothic furniture still crowded the dining-room. The two grand pianos had been left behind; one of them went to a Boy Scouts assembly hall, where it served the purpose of accompanying the boys when they were doing their physical exercises, the other was thrown on to a scrap-heap and eventually burned. So ended my musical ambitions, in farce and in flame. Sometimes I dream of those pianos, and their yellowing keyboards over which my fingers strayed, and sometimes across infinite distances I can hear the faint echoes of the melodies which I contrived – even those of the juvenile *étude* which won me the title of a 'young Chopin'. Such dreams are not conducive to spiritual repose, and I do not encourage them.

Even the drawing-room mantelpiece survived intact, faithfully reproduced as it had always been. Some of the vases were cracked, and one of the ebony elephants had been lost in transport. Otherwise nothing was changed. It was as though my mother's hands had stretched from the grave and guided Paul's fingers while he was arranging them. I no longer commented on this melancholy parade of rubbish, though there were times when I had the familiar urge to sweep it all away. But gradually I came to accept the mantelpiece, not for what it was, but for what it signified. It was another example of Paul's tributes to my mother's memory, his acceptance of the marriage vows which she had undertaken. When he placed a broken ornament on a strip of faded velvet he was not an elderly provincial vicar preparing the drawing-room for a tea-party with his parishioners. He was a man who had greatly suffered, but a man who had not let suffering destroy him – a man who was faithful unto death and beyond it. He was not concerned with ornaments, broken or unbroken. He was laying flowers on her grave.

III

'What did he die of?'

I cannot remember the precise hour or occasion of this question which I put to Paul; but it was shortly after the funeral, and we were standing in the little hall under one of the bogus family portraits.

'Starvation.'

Paul was very tired – too tired to give me a comfortable answer.

'Starvation?'

'So the doctor told me.'

But this, I thought, was ridiculous. None of our family had ever been rich, but there was *some* money, even in the poorest branches.

'I don't understand.'

'He died of starvation,' continued Paul, 'because he had no wish to live. It was as though he deliberately ordered his body to stop. He refused to feed himself, or to be fed.'

Himself? For the last time I ask ... 'Who was "himself"?'

I do not believe that it was 'himself' whom my father was refusing to acknowledge, but the spirit possessing him – a spirit born of alcohol, sustained and nourished by alcohol, preserved and kept from physical corruption by alcohol – as clearly as a hideous embryo in a glass jar, on the shelf of a medical museum. This was what had 'died'. This was what had flown out of the window of the shabby vicarage, through the faded curtains, leaving on the bed an elderly man, his eyelids closed and pressed down by a patient nurse.

And at long last his face – the face which had haunted me, terrified me, enraged me, followed me through all the twisted echoing, darkening corridors of life – was at peace. He lay in quiet repose and under the moustache there was the ghost of a smile. He had won.

Requiescat.

'I set it all to music' ∂❧

The piano piece published overleaf is the 'furious and disjointed *étude*' to which I referred in Chapter 5, Book II. Here I called it a 'musical curiosity', which it certainly is. The phrasing is almost non-existent, the pedalling is incomplete, and several bars, which I added later, are missing. But it seemed best to publish it as it was written, if only to illustrate my desperate efforts to make musical sense out of a life that was making no sense at all.

Should any professional pianist try it over, he might note that instead of 'Allegro agitato' it should be marked 'Allegro con fuoco', as in the twelfth *étude* of Chopin, to which of course it owes a great deal technically. I have never heard it myself, except in my head, for the simple reason that I have never had the technique to play it fast enough.

It is perhaps fitting that *Father Figure* should end with music, in the same way that my first book, *Prelude*, began with music, over fifty years ago.